SOLDIERS ON THE WALL

BOOT CAMP

Shellie Polk

First Printing: 2014

ISBN 978-0-578-13664-6

Shellie Polk
USA
29740 Charlotte Hall Road
Charlotte Hall, MD 20622
www.shelliepolk.com

"No one has yet figured out how to manage people into battle.

They must be led."

— Author Unknown

Dedication

This book is dedicated to my Lord and Savior Jesus for His glory.

Also, to the love of my life, my husband, Donald Polk, who has not always understood what I was seeing or telling him--but he has always listened, encouraged, loved, interceded, and supported me.

To my children and grandchildren who give me love, laughter and joy. They anchor me while continuing to fight for others in helping to release them from oppression. I love you: April, Summer, Autumn, Craig, Katie, Danielle, Natalie, Brittney, Haley & Sean. Also, my son, Donald, who went home to be with the Lord.

My awesome parents, Autumn & Harry Kraft, who provided love and a firm foundation of faith to build on.

I would like to thank my son, and artist, Craig Polk, for the illustrations in this book. And to my sister, Robin, who painstakingly proofed/edited this book.

To my sisters: Vickie, Susan, Harriet and Robin who have listened, taught, laughed, cried and prayed with/for me. They are a precious gift to me. And to the best brother and friend ever Harry.

Forward

Spiritual darkness is a reality that every Christian should become aware of. Regardless of your Church upbringing, this is one topic that many Churches discuss and debate. Shellie has poured her heart, her soul, and her experience into this written work. I have known Shellie for over 15 years and believe that her heart is to serve the body of Christ and to help create an awareness of the invisible enemy. I pray this book provokes you to search deeper the meaning of this Warfare!

Dr. Wilson Morales
Senior Pastor
Encounter Christian Center
Charlotte Hall, Maryland, USA

Introduction

My name is Shellie Polk, and I am an ordained minister of the Gospel of Jesus Christ. I am called as an Evangelist. I currently serve on the ministerial staff at Encounter Christian Center leading the Soldiers On The Wall Ministry.

God has impressed upon me that He wants to organize and restructure ministries in preparation for His expansions. He is ready to move the spiritual tent pegs out in His church.

Isaiah 54:2-3

"Enlarge the place of your tent; stretch your curtains wide, do not hold back; lengthen your cords, strengthen your stakes. For you will spread out to the right and to the left; your descendants will dispossess nations and settle in their desolate cities."

Time is short! We must, through prayer, hold the spiritual walls so as many people as possible can be saved. Lives are at stake and I do not want anyone's blood on my hands because I did not act by training soldiers in God's army.

My purpose is to reproduce leaders by teaching what I have personally experienced in spiritual warfare and evangelism. When I say I have seen something, I will be referring to things that I have seen either with my eyes open or with my eyes closed.

My current assignment is to train the Body of Christ into soldiers trained in spiritual warfare. I will try to impart to you what I have learned, and am still learning, in every spiritual battle I participate in.

I will endeavor to build from the basics of intercessory prayer to the more advanced; stay with me as we march thru these exercises towards becoming a fierce prepared army of intercessors.

This book will not go into the subject of personal deliverance, although this too is key in spiritual warfare.

I will stay focused on spiritual warfare and distinguishing "who" the spiritual enemy really is. There are so many various demonic groups functioning today in which Satan is their god. However, we are going to focus on the bigger enemy: the powers and principalities that they take direction from. God says our battle is not against flesh and blood but powers and principalities, so this will be the focus of this book.

When I was asked to restructure the intercessory prayer group at Encounter Christian Center, I did not give my answer right away. My first response was to pray and talk to the previous leaders of this ministry. I did not want to cause any hurt feelings that could possibly give Satan a foothold into our church. You don't want to start off building on polluted ground. Make sure the ground is clear of emotional debris.

I then asked God my usual question – "Why?" He impressed on me that this ministry was to be called **"Soldiers on the Wall,"** and that I was to train warriors into elite soldiers.

I asked Him for an assistant, and He gave me my long-time friend; I needed an "Aaron," just like Moses. Ask God for an armor bearer for your troop of soldiers. We work together as a troop of elite soldiers.

I was instructed by God to put out this "Call" to others:

"REPORT FOR DUTY!"

I spoke it and I wrote it, and others heard the cry of the Spirit.

I pray that you will form or regroup your prayer partners into a "Soldiers On The Wall" ministry, and you too will begin to storm the heavens while your church is holding services.

Expect resistance by the enemy in forming your group; he doesn't want anyone to pray or anyone to be saved.

Please be warned:

This is not a game! This is war, and you are in God's army.

Before going any further into this book, let's pray:

Father,

I have heard your "Call". Train me in the unseen war that I may serve as a Soldier On The Wall for Your glory. Open my spiritual ears, eyes and heart to be effective. It is written, whatever I bind on earth will be bound in the heavenlies and whatever I loose on earth will be loosed in the heavenlies. I bind any power or principality that would try to come against me while training, in the name of Jesus. I loose God's angels to surround me. By and thru Jesus I pray. Amen.

At the end of each chapter, I will give you room to write "NOTES" on what God is impressing upon you to discuss and pray over in your group of intercessors. All battles are different, so your battle strategy may be different from mine; pray and ask God for your strategy. Get your highlighter out and make notes throughout this training. If you seek God, you will find Him. This is just some of the building blocks you will use to restructure or start your individual prayer ministries. Build it the way God tells you to. I pray you get some useful material out of this book in the building of your prayer wall.

All scripture that I reference can be found in the New International or the American Standard Versions of the Bible unless otherwise noted, and definitions have been taken from Strong's Hebrew/Greek Dictionary.

Chapter 1 - Mission

All soldiers have a mission, a purpose for battle. As a spiritual soldier, your mission is:

Ezekiel 22:30

"I looked for someone among them who would build up the wall and stand before me in the gap on behalf of the land so I would not have to destroy it, but I found no one."

Isaiah 62:6

"I have posted watchmen on your walls, Jerusalem; they will never be silent day or night. You who call on the Lord, give yourselves no rest,"

You stand in the spiritual gap and hold the spiritual ground during your church service; you will be a **Soldier On The Wall**!

God is counting on us to be His body here on earth, to build up and hold the spiritual wall. This wall is made up of prayers, and we are here to defend it. You will learn how to do so.

Notice in Isaiah that we are told to "never be silent". We must speak the Word; the enemy cannot read our minds. We cannot rest while on duty. We are to be ready instantly when called to prayer.

The General for your troop of soldiers is your Pastor. We always answer to God first, and then to the Pastor. You must trust your Pastor and take direction from the leader that he/she appoints to lead your Soldiers On The Wall.

On August 2011, I saw a vision and the Lord told me,

"Tell my people time is short." I then saw the Antichrist was on his way, and he will come into the public arena. We don't have time to play at war anymore; the enemy knows his time is short. We need to give as many people as possible the opportunity to pray for salvation. We must hold the spiritual wall and take ground away from the enemy through prayer.

The Lord impressed upon me as I was praying that I should accept the restructuring of the intercessory prayer group to put out this "Call":

"God is calling His soldiers to REPORT FOR DUTY!"

The response in the spirit realm is why you have purchased this book and/or are attending a Soldiers On The Wall Boot Camp.

Time for boot camp!

Are you ready?

NOTES:

_____
_____
_____
_____
_____
_____
_____
_____
_____
_____
_____
_____
_____
_____
_____
_____
_____
_____
_____
_____
_____
_____
_____
_____
_____
_____

Reminder: Pray now before moving onto the next chapter.

Chapter 2 – Assignment

You know your Mission, so now what are your assignments/orders?

Here are a few:

-     You pray for the protection of your Pastor as he/she is used to bring forth God's Word.

-     You intercede on behalf of the lost and/or sick that the Lord will be sending into your church.

-     You stand alert while on duty and watch for any advancement of the enemy, you watch over the members of your church family.

You will be a highly trained soldier in the mighty, victorious army of God.

The enemy will always try to take out the Pastor because he/she is bringing forth the life changing Gospel of Jesus Christ. If you hear or see something happening to the Pastor, pray for protection for him/her.

Here are a few examples to look for:

-     he/she may lose their voice;
-     he/she may lose their place while reading;
-     he/she may lose their train of thought;
-     he/she may appear to lose physical strength.
-     The sound system may suddenly go crazy
-     The electronics stop functioning

YOUR PASTOR IS UNDER ATTACK!

You don't have to "see" in the Spirit to recognize an attack. God has given us eyes to see and ears to hear. Use your weapons and fight! We will go over some of the weapons available to you as a Soldier on the Wall.

Pray for the unsaved and sick people that the Lord will lead to your church. Pray for protection that they can hear the Word of God without distraction. Pray that their hearts are softened. Pray that their spiritual eyes are opened. Pray the Word!

When you see soldiers on guard, they are not in a casual posture. They stand alert and watch for anything unusual on the horizon. Your church may have a very valuable tool available to you --security cameras. (If you do not have this technology, use your eyes and ears by having someone in the sanctuary, another walking the halls watching and two praying where you have designated the prayer wall.)

Wherever the monitor is located, you will be able to see the various rooms in your church. That is where the Soldiers On The Wall should be praying during service. One person should be watching the monitor, and another one praying. You are working together as a troop of soldiers. You are not only praying for your Pastor, but also for the teachers. They are also bringing forth the Gospel to your children. If you see a disturbance in one of the rooms, pray. Switch watches so you stay alert on duty. Switch to watch the camera while the other soldier switches to pray.

You should also have a soldier with the gift of discernment in the sanctuary watching over the church. That person should sit in the back of the sanctuary so he/she can see the whole sanctuary. If that person sees or senses the enemy has breached the spiritual wall, they should pray and let the other soldiers know by getting up quietly and going to the prayer wall and immediately begin praying. Not a time for speculation!

You may be thinking that the enemy cannot come into the presence of God. NOT TRUE! Read the book of Job. The enemy goes before the throne of God to accuse us. He knows we are praying and he is testing the wall for any weaknesses. It could be someone was sent by the enemy to pray against your service.

You are called as God's warrior, but now you need to move into the realm of becoming God's Elite Soldier. And like all soldiers, you need boot camp. You may be a good soldier already, but you can always find a nugget of truth from someone else. You can do this! Nothing is impossible for our God. You will be highly trained.

NOTES:

_____

_____

_____

_____

_____

_____

_____

_____

_____

_____

_____

_____

_____

_____

_____

_____

_____

_____

_____

_____

_____

_____

_____

_____

_____

_____

Reminder: Pray now before moving onto the next chapter.

Chapter 3 - Purpose Of Battle

First things first, what is the purpose of battle:

Ephesians 6:10
"Finally, be strong in the Lord, and in his mighty power."

<u>You are nothing in a spiritual battle by your own strength</u>; the Lord Jesus already fought and won the battle. You remind the enemy of what Jesus did by shedding His blood on the cross and how He overcame death. You have the authority as His child to use His name. Just like at your physical birth you were given your family name to use, after your spiritual birth you now have the legal authority to use the name of Jesus. Jesus is the Word of God made flesh, use the Word of God to defeat the enemy.

You must be a born-again Christian to go onto the battlefield.

You do not have the authority without Jesus. You will not have the gift of discernment without the Holy Spirit living within you.

If you have never prayed and given your life to Jesus, **<u>DO IT NOW</u>**! Pray these words out loud:

Jesus,
I know that I am a sinner and I am sorry. I believe that You shed Your blood and died on the cross for me. I believe that on the third day You came back to life and ascended into Heaven and are seated at the right hand of the Father. I believe thru Your shed blood I am healed of all sickness and forgiven of my sins and I will spend eternity with You. I ask You to come into my life right now and be my best friend, my Lord and my Savior. I give You my life. Amen

If you just prayed that prayer, please go now to the section at the back of this book entitled "Now What?" it will explain in detail what just happened. Then continue your training.

If you have never prayed for the Baptism of the Holy Spirit, like on the day of Pentecost in the Book of Acts, let's pray now:

Father God,
I am asking by and thru Jesus that You fill me to overflowing with the Holy Spirit with evidence of the spiritual gifts as You would see fit to use through me. I ask this for Your glory. Equip me for battle. Amen

God is the only person who has the strength and the authority, but He lives in us!

"Greater is He who lives in us than he who lives in the world." (1John 4:4)

"He did not give us a spirit of fear, but of power, and of love, and a sound mind." (2Timothy 1:7)

The victory is the Lord's!

Do not think that you can defeat a demonic being in your own strength. Repeat after me,

"I am no match for a demon in my own strength!"

Let's look at the book of Acts to read an example of what happens when you try to take on a demon in your own strength:

Acts 19:11-16

"God did extraordinary miracles through Paul, so that even handkerchiefs and aprons that had touched him were taken to the sick, and their illnesses were cured and the evil spirits left them. Some Jews who went around driving out evil spirits tried to invoke the name of the Lord Jesus over those who were demon-possessed. They would say, 'In the name of the Jesus whom Paul preaches, I command you to come out.' Seven sons of Sceva, a Jewish chief priest, were doing this. One day the evil spirit answered them, 'Jesus I know, and Paul I know about, but who are you?' Then the man who had the evil spirit jumped on them and overpowered them all. He gave them such a beating that they ran out of the house naked and bleeding."

Once again repeat after me, **"I am no match for a demon in my own strength!"**

Did you also notice the demon said he knew **of** Paul? Demons communicate. I imagine their conversation went like this:

"That Saul who we had has now been saved and renamed Paul by Jesus. Don't get near him. He is a threat to anyone of us who come into contact with him."

You will become a threat to the demonic realm also. Praise God!

You stand your ground! Don't retreat because the victory is already assured by the work of Jesus on the cross. Do not let the enemy intimidate you; he will try anything to make you afraid. Look at little David facing the giant with only stones and a slingshot. Goliath intimidated all the other soldiers, but David knew the victory was the Lord's.

NOTES:

_____

_____

_____

_____

_____

_____

_____

_____

_____

_____

_____

_____

_____

_____

_____

_____

_____

_____

_____

_____

_____

_____

_____

_____

_____

_____

_____

_____

_____

_____

_____

Reminder: Pray now before moving onto the next chapter.

Chapter 4 - Purpose Of Armor

What is the purpose of armor?

Ephesians 6:11

"Put on the full armor of God, so that you can take your stand against the devil's schemes."

You must wear the armor of God while engaging the enemy. This armor was placed on you at the time of your salvation. You do not move, the enemy does!

Every day before you get out of bed, check each piece of the armor that God has given you through Jesus. Before I go into battle I check each piece of my armor to make sure it is secure. We are reminding ourselves that we are clothed in Jesus.

Here is a personal example as to why you need to check your armor:

One time I went into a home to pray with the owner because the family was under spiritual attack. I brought an armor bearer with me and I prayed with the owner for salvation before we attempted to dislodge the enemy from that home. I was scratched and bit on my ankle, spiritually not physically. (I felt it but saw no evidence of the attack) I asked God why that happened since I had never been physically attacked before in battle. His reply was, "you did not check your armor before going into that home." Before you leave home to stand on the prayer wall, check your armor.

We will go into detail on the pieces of your armor.

Be patient, it is coming.

NOTES:

_____
_____
_____
_____
_____
_____
_____
_____
_____
_____
_____
_____
_____
_____
_____
_____
_____
_____
_____
_____
_____
_____
_____
_____
_____
_____
_____
_____
_____
_____
_____
_____
_____

Reminder: Pray now before moving onto the next chapter.

Chapter 5 - Who Is The Enemy

Every soldier must know who or what the enemy is.

I underlined the words describing the enemy and looked them up in the Strong's Hebrew/Greek Dictionary. You need to know who the enemy is and how strategic Satan has his army lined up for battle. Demons move up in rank like any military power.

Let's break down the following verse:

Ephesians 6:12
[Using New American Standard version of the Bible for this word study]

"For our struggle is not against flesh and blood,

but against the <u>rulers</u>,

[Rulers: Arche, ar-khay, means chief (in various applications of order, time, place or rank. To be first in political or power rank.]

against <u>powers</u>,

[Powers: exousia, *ez-oo-see-ah,* in the sense of ability privilege – force – freedom – superhuman – token of control . Influence authority, jurisdiction, liberty, power, right and strength.]

against the <u>world forces</u> in this darkness,

[Forces: koamokrator, *kos-mok-rat-ore,* a world ruler an epithet of Satan] *against the <u>spiritual forces</u> of*

> [Spiritual Forces: pneumatikos *pnyoo-mat-sk-oa,* demonic spirits]

<u>*wickedness*</u> *in the*

> [Wickedness: poneria *pon-ay-ree-ah* depravity, malice, plots, sins, iniquity]

<u>*heavenly places.*</u> *"*

> [Heavenly places: scripture talks of Heaven 2 Corinthians 12:2 (3rd Heaven) where God's throne is and heavens space in between where demonic have power.]

Ephesians 6:12

<u>Rulers</u>: the top ranking, right beneath Satan, himself.

<u>Powers</u>: I focus on the word "superhuman" force. More than this human can do BUT not superhuman compared to Jesus, who already won this battle. They can take on any shape they want to put fear in you. These focus on geographical jurisdiction and influence the authority of the specific countries.

<u>World Forces</u> speaks for itself—Satan.

The next in rank: <u>spiritual forces</u>, these are the territorial demons. They are assigned specific territories in the geographical region assigned by Powers. Step up over the lowest demons.

<u>Wickedness</u>, the lowest ranking: demons. These have the assignments to oppress individuals.

There are levels in the atmosphere. If there is a third Heaven, there is the first and second. Scripture talks about battles and signs in the heavens (plural), but when scripture talks about the throne room of God (the third Heaven) the word is "Heaven". Singular usage.

The Lord showed me this in a vision and like scripture says, I am not sure if I actually went there spiritually or just in a vision, that is just how real it was. This is only part of the vision to demonstrate the heavenlies:

The Lord took me in His arms and took me thru the heavenlies. I am normally afraid of heights, but I wasn't then because He had me in His arms. I knew nothing could harm me in the demonic because of the Lord's presence. They didn't even come to my mind. The heavenlies are so vast, huge and beautiful. As we were approaching the third Heaven, I marveled at the brightness as we approached; it is a light that we cannot comprehend here on earth. There are no shadows because His light (glory) is everywhere at once.

The enemy may roam to and fro, but our God, who created everything, sees everything, and He is omnipresent. And His creation is spectacular.

NOTES:

_____
_____
_____
_____
_____
_____
_____
_____
_____
_____
_____
_____
_____
_____
_____
_____
_____
_____
_____
_____
_____
_____
_____
_____
_____
_____
_____
_____
_____
_____
_____
_____

<u>Reminder: Pray now before moving onto the next chapter.</u>

Chapter 6 - Armor Time!

It's time to put on the full armor of God piece by piece.

Ephesians 6:13-17

Ephesians 6:13

"Therefore, ***put on*** *the full armor of God, so that* ***when the day of evil comes****, you may be able to* ***stand your ground****, and after you have done everything, so stand.*

It is your choice to put on the armor or not. When you prayed for salvation, you made the choice to follow Jesus and was instantly clothed in the armor. You put on the Lord. You must check each piece to remind yourself of His protection.

We must put on the armor. Scripture also uses the words *"we must take up our cross and follow Him"* (Matthew 6:24).

Take up or put on are actions on our part. Notice also, when the day of evil comes we will be <u>involved</u> in the battle. After doing everything we can, we stand and do not move.

Ephesians 6:14

> "**Stand firm** then, with the **belt** of **truth** buckled around your waist, with the **breastplate** of **righteousness** in place,"

When the Lord repeats Himself he wants us to take notice. He says stand firm in verses 13 and then again in verse 14.

How do you stand firmly? If you stand with your feet together and knees locked, it is very easy for anyone to push you off balance.

Go ahead, stand up and take this stance. Do you feel the tension in your body? Ok, now sit down. This is usually the stance a person takes when they are afraid.

But if you stand one foot slightly ahead of the other and brace yourself in a determined stance, it is not easy, without shoving, to make you fall. Stand up and take a determined stance, feel the difference? Your confidence just skyrocketed! Now sit down. In this stance you show you are ready for battle, standing firmly. You are determined to stand your ground.

Put on the belt of truth. What is truth? Jesus is the truth!

John 14:6

"Jesus answered, 'I am the way and the <u>truth</u>, and the life. No one comes to the Father except through Me."

The belt protects your lower organs. It is a place for the next piece of armor to rest onto. It also holds other weapons when not in use.

What is the breastplate of righteousness? This piece covers your heart and vital organs. Roman breastplates had no protection at the back because retreat was not an option and it is not an option for you either. It was held in place by straps; think of these as the stripes Jesus took for you. Since Jesus endured that pain, we must and will have the courage to stand.

Be assured that you have the victory through Jesus; He already fought and won the ultimate battle. His righteousness or holiness covered you when you asked Him into your life. His shed blood makes you clean and holy in the sight of God.

Romans 5:19

"For just as through the disobedience of the one man [Adam] the many were made sinners, so also through the obedience of the one man [Jesus] the many will be made righteous."

Picture in your mind the most holy person you can think of. Have the picture?

Maybe you thought of Mother Theresa, the Pope, or Billy Graham...

God tells us that our righteousness is like filthy rags. You cannot obtain holiness on your own by any work or action you do on this earth. It is only through the work of Jesus on the cross and the Holy Spirit living within you that you can strive towards the holiness that pleases God.

All the people you brought to mind are Christians, but they could not achieve holiness in and of their own strength. The more time you spend with God, you are being transformed by the power of the Holy Spirit into the likeness of Jesus.

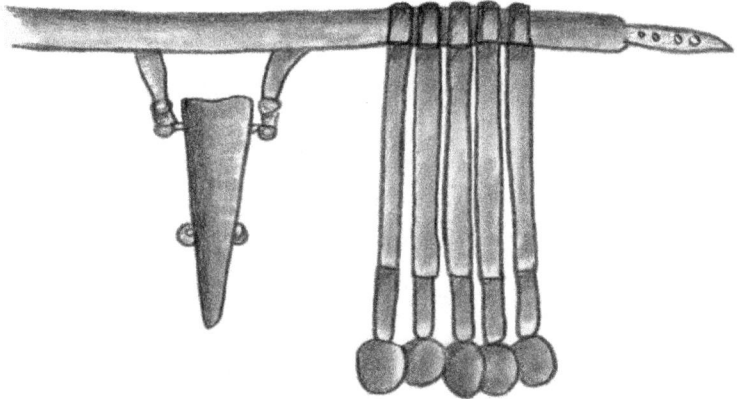

Ok, put your belt on. Stand up and hook that belt on now. I want you to close your eyes, and touch the **belt** of truth. Do you feel it spiritually? This belt anchors you. It is the truth.

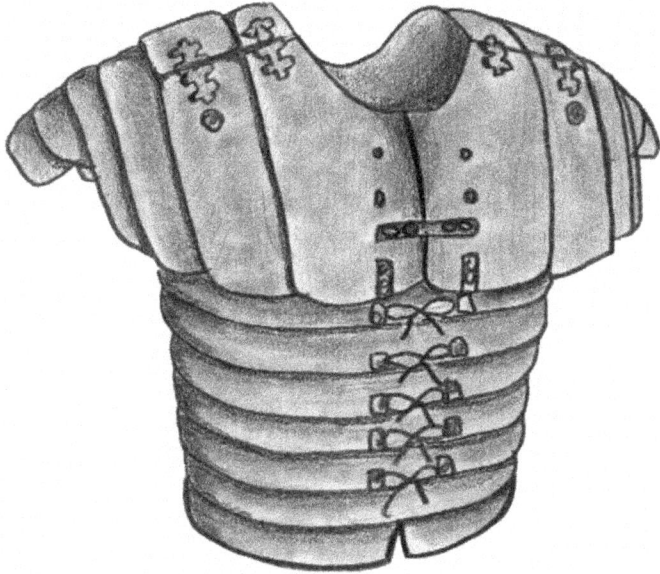

Remain standing. I want you to slip over your head the **breastplate** of **righteousness**. Close your eyes. Go ahead; no one is looking but God. He is showing you how to put it on. The breastplate of the Roman soldier had straps that fastened around the back to the front. This will remind you of the stripes that Jesus took. The whip tore His precious back and snaked around to the front of Him as He was tortured.

Did you see His holiness covering you over your head and then going down over to cover your heart? As you fastened the straps, did it remind you of the stripes He took for you? The blood of Jesus has washed you clean. His glory covers you. Now make sure it is fastened in place.

Ephesians 6:15

"and with your feet fitted with the readiness that comes from the gospel of peace."

Why does God fit your feet with the gospel of peace? He doesn't want us to stay in place and keep the salvation message to ourselves. He expects us to take it to the unsaved. You must walk out your own salvation with fear and trembling. *(Philippians 2:12)* This footwear has soles that can tread on snakes (Satan took on the appearance of a snake in the garden) *(Genesis 3:1)* and scorpions and we will not be harmed. *(Luke 10:19)* They keep us from slipping on anything the enemy puts in our path to try to make us fall. They keep us surefooted when walking through the valley of the shadow death because we will fear no evil. *(Psalm 23:4)* They help us to run the race of life.

I guess you know what I am going to ask you to do now. Yes, that's right, go ahead and lean over now and put on those sandals of the gospel of peace.

Now close your eyes and picture them, are they on securely? Okay - open your eyes.

Now you have put on most of the offensive pieces of armor; God is now going to give you defensive pieces to battle with.

Ephesians 6:16

"in addition to all this, take up the shield of faith, with which you can extinguish all the flaming arrows of the evil one.

What is faith? It is a belief that you trust. Here are a few insights into what the Word of God says about faith:

Matthew 9:2

"Some men brought to him a paralyzed man, lying on a mat. When Jesus saw their faith, he said to the man, 'Take heart, son; your sins are forgiven.'"

Jesus can see our faith by our actions.

Luke 7:50

"Jesus said to the woman, 'Your faith has saved you; go in peace."

Our faith saves us.

Romans 5:1

"Therefore, since we have been justified through faith, we have peace with God through our Lord Jesus Christ,"

We are justified by our faith.

Acts 26:18

> *"to open their eyes and turn them from darkness to light, and from the power of Satan to God, so that they may receive forgiveness of sins and a place among those who are <u>sanctified</u> by faith in me."*

We are sanctified by our faith in Jesus. So what does sanctified mean? In the Greek, the word is "hagios" which means holiness. We are separated from this world when we give our lives to Jesus; we are covered in His holiness. We are in this world but we are no longer a part of this world. We progress in this holiness (or sanctification) while we wait for the return of Jesus to take us home to Heaven, where we will be transformed into the likeness of Jesus. Holy, sanctified and totally separated from any presence of sin.

2 Corinthians 5:7

> *"for we live by faith, not by sight"*

It does not matter what we see, we focus on the unseen as though seen. Faith is seeing the unseen as though it has already been accomplished.

James 1:6

> *"But when you ask, you must believe and not doubt, because the one who doubts is like a wave of the sea, blown and tossed by the wind."*

We must ask in faith through Jesus without doubting. Doubt is the opposite of faith.

Faith comes by the hearing of God's Word. You can increase your faith by studying God's Word.

This shield is to block the flaming arrows the enemy will shoot at you.

Psalm 76:3

"There he broke the flashing arrows, the shields and the swords, the weapons of war."

The Holy Spirit will extinguish all flaming/flashing arrows; hold firmly onto that shield and you can protect any part of your body.

While acting as an intercessor for my Pastor who was teaching a class, I saw six spiritual arrows come half way through the wall of the classroom and then they were pulled back through the wall. The arrows were black, the Holy Spirit extinguished the fiery arrows and the shield of faith prevented them from projecting into the classroom.

You can make the prayer wall stronger by standing shoulder to shoulder with other soldiers on the wall holding your shields of faith in front of you.

Ancient soldiers, when out in the open, would make a circle and put their shields side by side to block an attack or put their shields over their heads like a roof to block the arrows from raining down upon them from above. In the Old West, settlers would circle their wagons to block their enemy from breaching their defense. The shield can be moved into many positions during battle. The Romans would soak their shields in water to extinguish flaming arrows. Our shield should be soaked in the Holy Spirit. The Shield of Faith is your first defensive piece of armor.

I guess you know the drill, stand and pick up your shield of faith.

Pray and ask the Holy Spirit to wet it down real good for you. Close your eyes and picture it. Feel the weight of it. Move it around: first it front, now to your side and above your head. Open your eyes, sit down and set it beside your chair.

Ephesians 6:17

"Take the **Helmet of Salvation**, and the **Sword** of the **Spirit**, which is the **Word of God**."

The Helmet of Salvation is an offensive and defensive piece of armor.

Offensive: It protects your head. Most importantly, it protects your brain and your thoughts. You are secure in Jesus that through His work on the cross and His resurrection you are saved. As a child of God, you are given authority to use the name of Jesus.

When you were saved, you first believed in your mind that Jesus died for you and that you were reconciled back to the Father through His Son, and Jesus asked the Father to send the Holy Spirit to live in you.

Defensive: The Holy Spirit teaches you about God. He brings recollection of scripture to your thoughts (your mind) in battle. In your mind, He reveals to you the enemy's plans and how to position yourself for battle.

All three persons in the God Head are present in any battle directing you in exactly what to say and do to see the victory.

Repeat after me: **<u>The Number One weapon of Satan is Fear!</u>**

God tells us repeatedly to "Fear Not" in His Word. *(Isaiah 41:10; Psalm 3:6; Psalm 27:3; Psalm 91:5…)*

If the enemy can get into your mind, he has a field day. God tells us to take control of our thoughts. He gives us the power to refuse thoughts and to turn our mind to what is good and pleasing to God.

Fear opens us up to so many things, both physical and mental. It harms us spiritually when we take our eyes (focus) off God.

When Peter took his eyes off Jesus and looked at the waves he began to sink in the water. When he was focused and looking at Jesus, He was walked on the water. He cried out to Jesus and the Lord caught him and helped him back into the boat.

If you take your eyes off of Him, He will rescue you also if you call out. Stay focused on Him! He did not give us a spirit of fear (comes from the enemy), but of power and a sound mind (comes from the Holy Spirit).

You must wear your helmet of salvation because the enemy uses your mind against you in battle. His number one weapon is fear.

God cannot hide the Word in your heart if you have not read His Word. Your sword is limited by the verses you have read. As you read the Word, you are sharpening your sword so it is ready for battle.

The Sword of the Spirit is your **Number One Weapon**.

You must read and study the Word (scripture).

Hebrew 4:12

> *"For the word of God is alive and active. Sharper than any double-edged sword, it penetrates even to dividing soul and spirit, joints and marrow; it judges the thoughts and attitudes of the heart."*

Now that is sharp!

In Revelation 2:16 Jesus is pictured with a double-edged sword coming from His mouth. He is the Word of God made flesh.

The sword as a weapon was and is used for up close and personal fighting. Jesus is our personal Savior and Lord. Satan and his army like to get up close when attacking.

I asked God, "why not a gun, so we don't have to get close?" He answered me, "we battle what is ancient, and that weapon did not exist then." Demons, or fallen angels, are ancient beings. They were created before man. We must learn to use the weapons He has provided for us. The Word always was and is and will always be.

Okay, you know the drill. Stand and pick up your helmet; put it on your head. Jesus is our head and we are the body. Close your eyes and picture the helmet that you have put on, secure it on your head with faith.

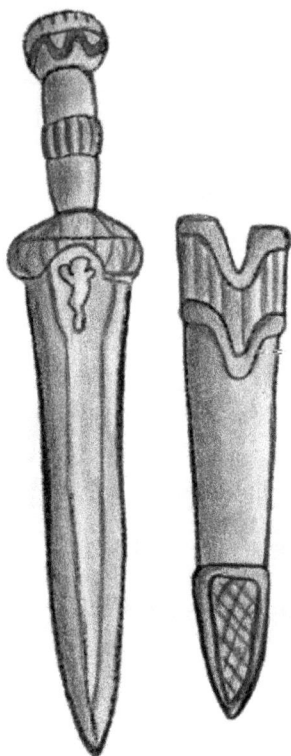

Now open up your eyes and pick up your sword. If you don't have your Bible next to you, then pretend to pick it up. Now close your eyes again and feel the weight of the sword. Feel the wisdom, knowledge and power that flows through that sword. Cling tightly to your sword and do not let the enemy take your sword away from you. Hide it in your heart.

Before you open your eyes I want you to touch and picture each part of your armor:

> The Helmet of Salvation;
> The Breastplate of Righteousness;
> The Belt of Truth;
> The Sandals of the Gospel of Peace;
> The Shield of Faith;
> and the Sword of the Spirit.

You are now fully armed.

You will be reinforcing the walls of your church and as in Nehemiah 4. The soldiers worked with one hand and held their sword in the other. You are building a wall of prayer, always with your sword ready to use in a moment's notice.

NOTES:

_____
_____
_____
_____
_____
_____
_____
_____
_____
_____
_____
_____
_____
_____
_____
_____
_____
_____
_____
_____
_____
_____
_____

Reminder: Pray now before moving onto the next chapter.

Chapter 7 - Prayer Time

You are fully armed, now it's time to pray.

Ephesians 6:18

"And pray in the Spirit on all occasions with all kinds of prayers and requests. With this in mind, be alert and always keep on praying for all the Lord's people."

•Do you have a prayer language? When you were Baptized in the Holy Spirit, did He give you a prayer language that you do not know?

This first occurred in the Book of Acts on the day of Pentecost. This is the Holy Spirit praying through you the perfect prayer. Use it. Allow Him to pray through you the perfect prayer.

•Stay alert and awake while standing watch on the prayer wall.

•You will be praying for your Pastor, the leadership, teachers, members, the sick, those oppressed by the demonic and the lost who will come into your Father's house seeking Him.

Let's look at *Acts 2:1-4*

"When the day of Pentecost came, they were all together in one place. Suddenly a sound like the blowing of a violent wind came from heaven and filled the whole house where they were sitting. They saw what seemed to be tongues of fire that separated and came to rest on each of them. All of them were filled with the Holy Spirit and began to speak in other tongues as the Spirit enabled them."

Study 1 Corinthians Chapter 12. Pray and ask God to give you the gift of tongues. Pray also for the greater gifts to benefit the body of Christ.

Speaking in tongues is used when you don't know what to pray, the Spirit groans through you the perfect prayer. Everyone can receive the gift of tongues for your prayer language.

This gift is also used by God in a church service, **ONLY IF** there is someone present who has the gift of interpretation. You can control this gift. You have to give control to the Holy Spirit to pray through you. He only uses this gift in a church service setting in an orderly fashion.

I use this gift while praying for individuals and He gives me the interpretation or direction in which to pray in English. I have asked Him to use me in whatever way He wants.

You will know it is God, when in many voices, someone's voice will rise up and the whole congregation becomes silent listening for the interpretation. When it is a word from God, it will apply to everyone present. It will be prophetic with a word of knowledge for that congregation.

You must use wisdom on when and how to use this gifting. Wonderfully, God says you only have to ask for wisdom and He will give it to you.

If you don't have this gift, use your own language. The enemy cannot read our minds. We must speak out loud for the enemy to hear how the sword is being used. Jesus responded when being tempted by Satan with: 'It Is Written, (then the scripture passage".) We must use His example because He overcame the enemy.

You must be on the alert and persevere through an attack. How can you be attacked while on duty? Getting sleepy, talking instead of praying, mind wandering to being hungry or thirsty, having to go to the bathroom, your phone ringing **(turn it to vibrate),** these are a few examples. Distraction is another weapon the enemy uses.

Have you seen the soldiers who stand guard in front of the castles of England? They stand at attention and are alert; no matter what anyone says or does they do not lose focus. Have you seen the soldiers guarding the Tomb of the Unknown Soldier in Arlington, Virginia? The same thing, they march back and forth and are always alert. You can learn lessons by watching soldiers.

Checklist before you go on duty to take your place on the prayer wall:

- Make sure your armor is in place;
- Eat breakfast or prayerfully fast;
- Bring your Bible and notebook with scriptures to use during battle;
- Turn your phone to vibrate;
- Bring a bottle of water;
- Be rested from a good night's sleep;
- Go into the sanctuary for praise & worship,
- Then take your place on the wall.

The singers went out before the soldiers in battle. There are many examples of praise and music as a weapon in the Bible.

A few examples:

The Walls of Jericho. *(Joshua 6:4)*

David with King Saul. *(1 Samuel 16:23)*

The Lord inhabits the praises of His people. His presence is ushered in through praise. Bring that praise and worship to the prayer wall.

NOTES:

_____

_____

_____

_____

_____

_____

_____

_____

_____

_____

_____

_____

_____

_____

_____

_____

_____

_____

_____

_____

_____

_____

_____

_____

_____

_____

_____

_____

_____

_____

Reminder: Pray now before moving onto the next chapter.

Chapter 8 - Protect Your Leader/General

Ephesians 6:19

"Pray also for me, that whenever I speak, words may be given me so that I will fearlessly make known the mystery of the gospel,"

Pray during the week, that your Pastor will hear exactly what God wants preached.

Pray for him/her and for his/her family's health and for protection from distractions.

Pray for leaders to follow and help in whatever way they can.

Pray for the teachers to hear the voice of God.

Pray that we move as ONE Body!

The enemy likes to attack the voice of a Pastor. Pray protection and refreshment of his/her body. Fear is a weapon used by the enemy to try to stifle the boldness the Pastor needs to reach the lost and to feed the Word of God to the sheep who are hungry.

Pray we are one body. We want our Pastors and our teachers to be used to lead others into salvation. Expect the enemy to fight to keep any person he can from coming to salvation.

Pray for protection over those in the building presenting the gospel of Christ.

Pray for God to give revelation knowledge of the Word to your Pastor and your teachers. That God will show the Pastor the needs of the congregation and the teachers the needs of every child and student.

Pray that those in ministry will overflow with the power of the Holy Spirit to instill hope, peace and joy into the Body.

We want the Body to be free from fear and all the physical and mental symptoms that are caused from fear and ignorance of the state of their soul.

Pray that our ministry leaders will be bold and speak the truth in love. Some will plant and some will reap. You are protecting the ground for planting and reaping.

You are part of an elite troop of soldiers being used for God's glory.

NOTES:

_____
_____
_____
_____
_____
_____
_____
_____
_____
_____
_____
_____
_____
_____
_____
_____
_____
_____
_____
_____
_____
_____
_____

Reminder: Pray now before moving onto the next chapter.

Chapter 9 - Prayer Is The Answer

•Do you want to reach the unsaved and see them give their lives to Jesus? **We must pray!**

•Do you want to see people delivered? **We must pray!**

•Do you want to see people healed? **We must pray!**

Churches that are reaching the lost (not just those sheep who are leaping from one shepherd to another) are praying churches.

I am guilty of not going to prayer meetings. How many years did Pastor have weekly prayer meetings and I did not attend? I was lazy and disobedient in my spirit.

I have changed and you can also. The Lord asked me in 2013 for my calendar. Since then, I am now ready to go at any time to pray for someone or to take a call 24/7 to pray with someone. My phone is next to my bed; you too, be available to pray.

We all must be ready for prayer at a moment's notice. When we say we will pray, make sure that you pray. Keep a prayer journal and write down what you have committed to pray for so that you will remember.

I don't want any of us to say, "I will be praying for you." I want to hear, "Okay, can I pray with you now?" When someone asks for prayer on a social media page or in person, PRAY!

Most Christians have no idea how to pray. We must teach them and every one of us has a different prayer style because we are all so different. There is not any right or wrong way to pray. We are boldly going into the throne room of God to talk to our Father on behalf of one of His children. The best way to learn how to pray is to be among praying people and then you will learn naturally by observing.

When I was first saved and my church would have a prayer meeting, I would go sit next to the oldest person and listen. It was incredible to hear the closeness of that mature Christian's prayers to God. I would go to prayer groups to pray in agreement with whatever was being prayed.

One night I was asked to pray for a very mature Christian woman who had arthritis. I was so frightened and intimidated to pray. All I said was, "Lord touch and heal (name) in Jesus' name. Amen" I know my Father in Heaven was so proud of me for overcoming my fear.

Baby steps turn into bold steps.

You are a trained soldier. Protect His sheep.

Expect the lost not fitting into the "church people" mold. The Lord tells us to feed and love them as they come to us. He will do the cleaning and changing into His image. Your motto should be as it is at Encounter Christian Center, "It is okay not to be okay."

The church is a safe haven for the injured and in most cases, injuries are very messy.

NOTES:

_____
_____
_____
_____
_____
_____
_____
_____
_____
_____
_____
_____
_____
_____
_____
_____
_____
_____
_____
_____
_____
_____
_____
_____
_____
_____
_____
_____
_____
_____
_____
_____
_____
_____

Reminder: Pray now before moving onto the next chapter.

Chapter 10 - Teach Me To Pray - Lord's Prayer

Teach me to pray; the disciples asked Jesus this same request.

Let's use the Lord's Prayer as an outline to learn how to pray:

Matthew 6:8

"*Do not be like them; for your Father knows what you need before you ask him.*"

Wow, just like in the same manner we see that our own child wants a drink, we teach them to "say please", the Father wants us to ask also. He wants to interact with us.

Write your own personal example.

Your Example:

_____

_____

_____

_____

_____

_____

_____

_____

_____

_____

_____

Matthew 6:9

"This, then, is how you should pray: 'Our Father in heaven, hallowed be your name,'"

We are directing our prayer to our Father, who is in Heaven and He is to be shown reverence. He is holy. We are praising and worshiping Him.

My Example:

Father,
I come before You. I love You, Lord. Thank You for hearing my prayer.

The Message Bible translation is this: *'Our Father in heaven, reveal who you are. "*

I am addressing Him and I am spiritually entering before Him sitting on His throne in Heaven.

I am telling Him how much I love Him.

I am worshiping Him for who He is and I am praising Him for all that He has done for me.

The Message Bible translation says, *"reveal who you are".*

What a concept! Every time we talk to Him, He is revealing who He is to us.

Your Example:

_____

_____

_____

_____

_____

Matthew 6:10

"*your kingdom come, your will be done, on earth as it is in heaven.*"

The Message Bible translation says, "*Set the world right; Do what's best —as above, so below.* "

We are lining ourselves up with God's will. We want what He wants.

My Example:

Father,
I come before You. I love You Lord. Thank You for hearing my prayer. **Lord, You say that You watch over Your Word to perform it** *(Jeremiah 1:12)*

[I am reminding Him of His Word, I am here on earth lining up with Heaven's position because the Word is truth.]

Your Example:

_____
_____
_____
_____
_____
_____
_____

Matthew 6:11

"Give us today our daily bread,"

The Message Bible translation says, "*Keep us alive with three square meals.*"

We are asking for God's provision of nourishment for our physical bodies. He always provides for His children's needs.

My Example:

Father,
I come before You. I love You, Lord. Thank You for hearing my prayer. Lord, You say that You watch over Your Word to perform it. *Father, You said not to worry about what I eat or drink. Lord, I really need groceries and I trust that You will provide.*

He, our Heavenly Father, is our Provider. As parents, we always provide meals for our children and He will do the same. Sometimes we eat at home, sometimes we eat at a family member's home. Is our church not our family also? So, if we are in need of food, can we not ask for food in our Father's house?

Example:

Many years ago I was out of work because of having had surgery on both hands. I was not allowed back to work until I could perform at 100%, but I was only functioning at about 80%. We were a family that needed two incomes and we were struggling. I looked in my pantry and I had no food and two young children. I prayed about the situation to God. Then there was a knock at my door; a family member had brought me groceries. I said, "You can't afford to do this". The family member said, "Don't you remember years ago when you gave me money for groceries? Well I am doing the same." Praise God!

I was volunteering during the day at the church and a man would bring day-old bread to the church. That bread sustained us during this same time. God will provide; don't let your pride make you stumble -- someone in an act of obedience is being used of the Lord. I know God blessed that family member for feeding us.

Your Example:

_____
_____
_____
_____
_____
_____
_____
_____

Matthew 6:12

"And forgive us our debts, as we also have forgiven our debtors. "

The <u>Message</u> Bible translation says, *"Keep us forgiven with you and forgiving others.*

We do not have a choice, if we ourselves are forgiven, we must forgive others.

My Example:

Father,
I come before You. I love You, Lord. Thank You for hearing my prayer. Lord, You say that you watch over Your Word to perform it. Father, You said not to worry about what I eat or drink. Lord, I really need groceries and I trust You to provide. ***Lord, You know sister (so and so) has really hurt me, help me to forgive her as You have forgiven me.***

It is not easy to forgive. We must take the first step and ask God to help us to forgive. Then the next step will be to start praying blessings over the person who hurt us. <u>Forgiveness is not an option.</u>

As stated in *Matthew 6:14-15:*

"For if you forgive other people when they sin against you, your heavenly Father will also forgive you. <u>But if you do not forgive others their sins, your Father will not forgive your sins.</u>" (Emphasis mine)

Wow, you better soften that hard heart or injured heart and forgive.

I once thought I could never forgive the woman who hurt mentally and physically my son as a toddler. I was filled with rage and hate concerning her. But God kept putting her physically right in front of me; first in my car while driving and she was in the car in front of me. I prayed and was shaking because I wanted to run her off the road. Then while in the grocery store, I had to walk out and leave my groceries. Then I was at my child's school; I let her walk past me. He kept putting her there before me until I began praying asking Him to help me to forgive her.

This was a long process; years, in fact. First, I began feeling sorry for her; thinking she was mentally ill. Then I was able to ask God to forgive me for my feelings of rage and hate. I wanted to forgive her. I also asked Him to heal her mentally/emotionally: whatever her problem was and to save her. It was a long process that just about ate me alive until I forgave her.

Guess what? As I was working on this book, God put her at the ball field and all this rage welled up within me. I hadn't truly forgiven her. So I have repented and prayed once again to forgive her. Recently, I have seen her two more times with no negative reaction. It may be an on-going process to reach forgiving a person; but we must forgive.

Your Example:

_____
_____
_____
_____
_____
_____
_____
_____
_____

Matthew 6:13

"And lead us not into temptation, but deliver us from the evil one,"

<u>The Message</u> Bible translation says, *"Keep us safe from ourselves and the Devil. You're in charge! You can do anything you want! You're ablaze in beauty! Yes. Yes. Yes."*

Ask for protection from temptations and attacks from the devil. Recognize who is in charge and how wonderful His perfect will is.

My Example:

Father,

I come before You. I love You, Lord. Thank You for hearing my prayer. Lord, You say that You watch over Your Word to perform it. Father, You said not to worry about what I eat or drink. Lord, I really need groceries and I trust You to provide. Lord, You know sister (so and so) has really hurt me, help me to forgive her as You have forgiven me. *Father, I ask that You put a hedge of protection around me and my family from the financial attacks the enemy is bringing against me. You are my Provider. I thank You for answering my prayer. I ask by and through Jesus. Amen*

This was my example of how I would pray the Lord's prayer. Now write your version.

YOUR EXAMPLE:

_____

_____

_____

_____

_____

_____

_____

_____

_____

_____

_____

_____

_____

_____

_____

_____

_____

_____

_____

NOTES:

_____

_____

_____

_____

_____

_____

_____

_____

_____

_____

_____

_____

_____

_____

_____

_____

_____

_____

_____

_____

_____

Reminder: Pray now before moving onto the next chapter.

Chapter 11 - Teach Me To Pray - Supplication Prayer

What exactly is the "Prayer of Supplication"?

This means to ask God for something (petition) for someone else or for ourselves.

Philippians 4:6

"Do not be anxious about anything, but in every situation, by prayer and petition, with thanksgiving, present your requests to God."

My Example:

Father,
I come to You lifting Sean up to You. Lord, by Your stripes we are healed and I ask that You heal Sean of high cholesterol. Thank You for healing him. In Jesus' name I pray. Amen.
This is the most often used/requested type of prayer.

Someone may ask you to pray for them. Be it for healing, a job, a home, their children etc...

In my example, you see that I am addressing the Father, then, I am calling out the person's name that I am petitioning Him on behalf. Did you notice how I am praying His Word back to Him? I am being specific in my request. I am thanking Him in advance. And I am acknowledging that I can only come to Him through my Savior Jesus.

All three persons of the Trinity are active in our prayers. We are talking to the **Father.** We come through the **Son** into the throne room (Jesus said that whatever we ask in His name will be done by the Father). The **Holy Spirit** gives us the words to pray and He carries us into the presence of the Father.

Okay, let's have you try a prayer of supplication. You probably have a list of people you are praying for, including yourself. So go ahead and write a Supplication Prayer.

YOUR EXAMPLE:

_____

_____

_____

_____

_____

_____

_____

_____

_____

_____

_____

_____

_____

_____

_____

_____

_____

_____

NOTES:

_____

_____

_____

_____

_____

_____

_____

_____

_____

_____

_____

_____

_____

_____

_____

_____

_____

_____

_____

_____

_____

_____

Reminder: Pray now before moving onto the next chapter.

Chapter 12 - Teach Me To Pray - Salvation Prayer

John 3:5-6

"Jesus answered, 'Very truly I tell you, no one can enter the kingdom of God unless they are born of water and the Spirit. Flesh gives birth to flesh, but the Spirit gives birth to spirit."

Romans 10:9-10

"If you declare with your mouth, 'Jesus is Lord,' and believe in your heart that God raised him from the dead, you will be saved. For it is with your heart that you believe and are justified, and it is with your mouth that you profess your faith and are saved."

This is the most important prayer we will ever pray individually or it's our highest honor to lead someone in the Salvation Prayer. This prayer changes someone for eternity.

In the gospel of John, Jesus is telling us about two separate births. The one of water is when you are born of your Mother. You were protected within a bag of water and the same water aided in your delivery. The second birth is by the Spirit; this time it is your choice. Your rebirth is by the Spirit. You are a new creation in Jesus, the old self is gone and you are brand new; all your sins are forgiven.

Romans tell us why it is important to confess with your mouth:

Satan cannot read our mind; we must speak out loud into the atmosphere. When we speak with our mouths, we are telling Satan; I reject you and I am now following Jesus; at that moment you are saved.

Remember the helmet of salvation protects your mind. You cannot speak if your mind is not engaged. Jesus is our head covering. A helmet is hard and strong; so is our Lord.

Take note in Romans that the moment you believe in your heart, His holiness starts to cover you. Remember the breastplate of righteousness? It covers your heart! No covering on the back because when you put your hand to the plow you do not look back but forward. The plow is before you, move straight ahead, because if you turn to look back, your path becomes crooked. So no looking back, eyes forward.

Here are the important elements of the Salvation Prayer:

- Recognize that you are a sinner and need a Savior.

- Believe in your heart that Jesus died and shed His blood (as the perfect sacrifice) for your sins so that you can stand before the Father washed clean.

- Believe that He rose from the grave (came back to life) thus conquering sin and death.

- He ascended into Heaven so we too will live eternally with the Father.

- Ask Him into your life as your Savior and Lord. Confess that He is God.

- Thank Him for saving you.

So how do you lead someone in the Salvation Prayer?

Tell the person that you will feed them the words, but they need to repeat them after you. Make sure you go **slowly** because they are usually very emotional and nervous approaching the Lord asking to be saved.

My Example:

Jesus,
I know that I am a sinner and I am sorry. I believe that You died on the cross for me. I believe through Your shed blood I am forgiven of all my sins and that You took all of my sicknesses. I believe that You rose from the grave, went back to Heaven and are alive. I ask You to come into my heart and be my best friend, my Savior and my Lord. Thank You. Amen

Remind the person that their name is now written in the Lamb's Book of Life; that all the angels are cheering because they just prayed. Tell them that they are a new creation through Jesus. The old is gone and the new has begun. Rejoice with them!

Encourage them to start reading their Bible so they can get to know Jesus. Ask them if you can pray a blessing over them. Then pray and ask God to bless them, (the Holy Spirit will give you the words to pray--trust Him.)

Okay, same drill, write out how you will lead someone in the Salvation Prayer.

YOUR EXAMPLE:

_____

_____

_____

_____

_____

_____

_____

_____

_____

_____

_____

_____

_____

NOTES:

_____

Reminder: Pray now before moving onto the next chapter.

Chapter 13 - Teach Me To Pray - Warfare Prayer

Matthew 16:18-19

> *"And I tell you that you are Peter, and on this rock I will build my church, and the gates of Hades will not overcome it. I will give you the keys of the kingdom of heaven; whatever you bind on earth will be bound in heaven, and whatever you loose on earth will be loosed in heaven."*

Memorize this scripture because you will use it a lot in warfare prayer.

In warfare you command the demonic. Jesus has given you authority.

When (not "if" because when people become saved, there will be attacks) there is an attack, we are assured that the devil will not overpower us.

Jesus has given us His authority to bind and to loose in His name.

My Example:

I bind you spirit of _____ in the name of Jesus! I command you to leave in the name of Jesus! *[Matthew 16:19 I will give you the keys of the kingdom of heaven; whatever you bind on earth will be bound in heaven, and whatever you loose on earth will be loosed in heaven.]*

Demons are named by their assignment or weapon they are using:

stubborn [*Deuteronomy 2:3*],

deaf and mute [*Mark 9:25*],

distraction, anger, depression, infirmity, divination/familiar [*Acts 16:16-18*],

stupor [*Romans 11:8*].

Jesus once asked a demon's name and the answer was Legion.

[*Mark 5:9* - "Then Jesus asked him, 'What is your name?' 'My name is Legion,' he replied, 'for we are many.'"]

Example:

I loose the holy warring angels in Jesus' name. [*Matthew 26:53 & Revelation 12:7*]

Example:

I loose the fire of God upon you. [*2 Kings 1:12*]

I have used all of these prayers in battle. I have always prayed to bind in battle. Once I was in an intense battle and I said, "I bind you in the name of Jesus!" Saw the demonic just slow down. I then heard the Holy Spirit say, "Finish the scripture!" I then said, "I loose the fire of Heaven upon you"; and saw a ball of fire hit and destroy the demonic.

You must know the Word of God. Read it and the Holy Spirit will hide it in your heart to be used when needed.

Let's practice some.

Here is the setting --

You are watching the security cameras (if you do not have security cameras, have a prayer warrior in the sanctuary watching) and Pastor is getting ready for the altar call. You see ushers coming in and out of the sanctuary.

What spirit is at work here? Distraction. Pray against it now.

_____
_____
_____
_____
_____
_____
_____
_____
_____
_____
_____
_____
_____
_____
_____
_____
_____
_____
_____

Here is the setting --

You are watching the security cameras and you see in a classroom two children arguing. (If you do not have security cameras, the intercessor monitoring the hallway sees or hears.)

What spirit is at work here?   Anger. Pray against it now.

_____
_____
_____
_____
_____
_____
_____
_____
_____
_____

Here is the setting --

Pastor is explaining about salvation and you see someone, cross his or her arms and look up.

What spirit is at work here? Unbelief, pride or maybe anger. Trust the Holy Spirit to prompt you how to pray. Pray against it now.

_____
_____
_____
_____
_____
_____
_____
_____
_____
_____

Here is the setting --

You see a person on the back row crying through the service.

How are you going to pray? Depression, grief, sickness, there could be many reasons for this circumstance. I would pray comfort and peace for the person but always go with the prompting of the Holy Spirit. Practice praying comfort and peace now.

_____

_____
_____
_____
_____
_____
_____
_____
_____
_____
_____
_____
_____
_____
_____
_____
_____
_____
_____
_____

Do you see why the security cameras are such a valuable prayer tool? (If you do not have cameras, your intercessors are just as valuable.) God says WATCH and pray.

NOTES:

_____

Reminder: Pray now before moving onto the next chapter.

Chapter 14 - Teach Me To Pray - Conclusion

There are so many different types of prayers. I have only touched on a few different types. You will discover more in your prayer life.

The **key** to all prayer is **Jesus**. He is the Word made flesh. Because of what He did we can approach the Father at any time. We have the Holy Spirit living in us to direct us in prayer.

God moves when someone asks in prayer. You are standing in the gap for those who cannot or do not know how to pray.

You are a Soldier On The Wall always watching and praying.

NOTES:

_____

_____

_____

_____

_____

_____

_____

_____

_____

_____

_____

_____

_____

_____

_____

_____

_____

_____

_____

_____

Reminder: Pray now before moving onto the next chapter.

Chapter 15 - Excerpts from "Fresh Wind, Fresh Fire" By Jim Cymbala

I highly recommend reading Fresh Wind, Fresh Fire, by Jim Cymbala. It will encourage and excite you. In this chapter, I will be. citing from his book

When a church starts to pray this is what can happen:

We started to think of ourselves as a "Holy Ghost emergency room" where people in spiritual trauma could be rescued" *{pg. 29}*

Wouldn't it be wonderful to be a Holy Ghost emergency room? I can picture "Emergency Room" entrance above every sanctuary door.

Doctor on duty: the Holy Ghost. WOW!

This is what I experienced in August of 2011 at a prayer meeting:

I saw the women present at the meeting, in a vision battling during the Praise & Worship. These women were some fierce soldiers for Christ. They weren't just singing to the Lord, they were in battle pushing through to the throne room of God.

After the Praise & Worship, we were asked to take a mat and lay on the floor; the visiting evangelist from Korea came and ministered individually to each person.

I saw in the spirit, the Holy Spirit as a mist going between each mat where women were laying, hovering over each one. I thought this looks like a battlefield hospital; all the people lined up on the floor with the Lord touching and ministering to each woman. It was a Holy Ghost Emergency Room!

"Prayer cannot truly be taught by principles and seminars and symposiums. It has to be born out of a whole environment of felt need. If I say, 'I ought to pray,' I will soon run out of motivation and quit; the flesh is too strong. I have to be driven to pray." *{pg. 49}*

You must ask God to give you an unquenchable thirst for lost souls. To have a hunger like no other to see the hand of God move in every service of your church.

Let's pray:

Father,
I ask that You set a fire in my soul with an unquenchable thirst for more of You and to see people saved, healed and delivered. Lord, overwhelm me with Your presence in every service. Everywhere I go, use me to witness about You. Open my eyes, ears and heart to do Your work every day. By and through Jesus I ask. Amen.

There are several statements *{pg. 58}* that struck me deep in my heart:

• **"prayer begets revival, which begets more prayer."**
• **"The Holy Spirit is the Spirit of prayer."**
• **"If we don't want to experience God's closeness here on earth, why would we want to go to heaven anyway?"**

Do you **really, really, really** want revival?

Then you must **really, really, really** get serious about prayer.

The Holy Spirit lives in each of us and He prays through us. He prompts us to pray. Do we always listen?

There have been times, I am ashamed to admit, that the Lord woke me up in middle of the night and I knew He wanted me to get up to pray. I told Him I was too tired and went back to sleep.

Now I am on duty 24/7. Will you also pray and ask God to put you on His 24/7 Call List?

Let me share with you about the night the Lord called my cell phone:

My niece was in over her head in a spiritual battle and the Lord told her to stop praying with her friend and to call me. But she didn't. Then He woke up my sister (her mother) and prompted her to call me; but she laid there thinking, "Shellie is tired. I don't want to call her at 3:00 in the morning."

Soooooooo, my phone rang. I got up out of bed and went in the kitchen to answer the phone. My sister's name was listed on the caller I.D. screen. I called her back. She told me she did not call me and told me what she had been thinking. So we began to intercede for her daughter.

I faced, in a vision, two very high demonic powers that were coming against my niece. The Holy Spirit instructed me how to blow them up. "How?" you may be thinking. The Blood of Jesus. I then called and talked with my niece. I told her: if she is under attack and needs reinforcements, then she needs to call for help. After praying, I looked at my phone's call log and my sister's name was not listed.

Nothing is impossible for God! If the finger of God can write on a wall in Old Testament times, the same finger can dial a phone. Did you notice He told both of them to "call" me and they didn't. So, He did! Amen!

{pg. 59} I thought this statement was very sad and thought how disappointed God must feel with His children:

"I have talked with pastor after pastor, some of them prominent and 'successful,' who have told me privately, 'Jim, the truth is, I couldn't have a real prayer meeting in my church. I'd be embarrassed at the smallness of the crowd. Unless somebody's teaching or singing or doing some kind of presentation, people just won't come. I can only get them for a one-hour service, and that only once a week."

Wow! Does this sound familiar?

As God's soldiers, we need to prepare the spiritual ground for revival. We must pray on the wall not only the one hour each Sunday. Start having prayer meetings. Start small and build your spiritual muscles to hold the prayer wall for longer periods of time. (Monthly, every other week, and then weekly.)

Watch out! A spiritual explosion is getting ready to happen to blow the enemy out of your area.

When revival truly begins it will be daily ongoing as long as the Lord honors us with His presence.

{pg. 96} "These people had already been filled with the Holy Spirit on the Day of Pentecost (Acts 2), but here they sensed a new need. God met them with a new infusion of power.'

'I am well aware that Christians disagree today on whether the infilling (baptism, empowerment) of the Spirit is a part of the salvation 'package' or a separate, subsequent experience. Long and intense discussions go on about that. Whatever you or I believe, let us admit that this passage shows bona fide Christians experiencing a fresh infilling. The apostles didn't claim they already had everything they needed. Now that they were under attack, they received fresh power, fresh courage, fresh fire from the Holy Spirit."

'Our store of spiritual power apparently dissipates with time. Daily living, distractions, and spiritual warfare take their toll. We need, in the words of Paul used in Ephesians 5:18 to 'be always being filled with the spirit'"

I believe there are two separate experiences.

The first: When we pray for salvation, the Holy Spirit comes into us and is with us.

The second: As on the day of Pentecost, there is the Baptism of the Holy Spirit:

Picture yourself as a glass of chocolate milk. Take the glass pour in the milk, then add the chocolate. Is that chocolate milk? Yes, but the chocolate has sunk to the bottom of the glass.

Now, when you ask The Father through Jesus to fill you with the Holy Spirit, it is like the Father taking His hand and stirring you up so that the chocolate is flowing through the milk.

This time is often when you will receive your prayer language. You are completely (with your whole being) asking and allowing the Holy Spirit to move through you as His vessel. He will use you in the gifts as you allow Him to move through you.

God knows when you are ready.

I prayed for months before I was filled with the Holy Spirit. It took so long because there was a part of me that was afraid. God is a loving Father and He will wait until you truly want the power of God.

Then, the next day while I was driving and praising God, I said a few words in a language I didn't understand. I said, "Did You hear that God?" I started laughing and then said, "that's You, of course you heard that!"

The gifts come over time. Prayer groups are an excellent place to use your gifts. All gifts are to be used to build up the Body of Christ, not for our enjoyment, even though He does allow us to feel good when we are used to help one of His children. That is His reward to us for being obedient.

Let me caution you: when God tells you something, **say it exactly as He told you.** To embellish at all is lying. Exaggeration is the same as lying.

How can you receive this infilling or baptism?

Praying by yourself (like the prayer in the beginning of this book) or by asking someone to lay hands on you to receive the infilling of the Holy Spirit. *(Acts 19:6)*

You must really want His power, believing, and He will fill you. The enemy will use doubt to discourage you. Don't allow him to steal your gifts. Keep praying until you are filled.

The Lord calls them gifts, like a present; but we don't own a particular gift. Our gift is a privilege to be used by the Lord in whatever capacity He wants to benefit another person's needs. The Holy Spirit lives in us, but we don't own Him. He is God and no one owns God.

{pg. 173} "He meets us in the moment of battle. He energizes us when there is an enemy to be pushed back."

{pg. 181} "Whenever God stirs us to establish his kingdom in a new place, the enemy is sure to taunt us. The devil always tries to convince us that we've tackled too much this time and we'll soon be humiliated."

God will always meet you on the battlefield. It is His battle.

When I get a call in middle of the night, I am instantly awake and ready. After the battle, the Lord allows me to go right back to sleep.

Make yourself available to pray 24/7. Give your phone number to those people that God brings to you for help. You are a Soldier On The Wall, ready at all times to pray.

The enemy does not want this type of ministry because he knows the Lord is expanding and/or taking back spiritual territory. The enemy is comfortable with small growth as long as we leave those he has deceived alone.

When the Holy Spirit starts drawing the lost to your church, you will, at times, have to hold the wall by force. The enemy will test the wall for weaknesses. Cover each other in prayer.

Expect attacks and ask one another for prayer to cast the enemy away. Praise God! You are standing! When you start pushing the territorial spirits out of your area, there will be a battle. They have held their ground for a long time and they don't give up without a fight. That is why we have a spirit of power and not fear. God says over and over, *"fear not!"* (emphasis mine.)

NOTES:

_____

_____

_____

_____

_____

_____

_____

_____

_____

_____

_____

_____

_____

_____

_____

_____

_____

_____

_____

_____

_____

_____

_____

_____

_____

_____

_____

_____

_____

_____

Reminder: Pray now before moving onto the next chapter.

Chapter 16 - What Weapons Are Available?

Praise, Singing, Worship:

•Praise: *Leviticus 19:24* (offering of praise)

•Singing: *1 Chronicles 16:9, Nehemiah 12:46, Hebrews 13:15, Revelation 19:5*

•Worship: First of the commandments,
"You shall have no other gods before me." *Exodus 20:3, Psalm 2:11, John 4:24, Philippians 3:3, Revelation 4:10*

Praise & Worship - Singers always went before the soldiers into battle. God inhabits the praises of His people. The enemy cannot stand singing and praising the Lord.

Praise & Worship is a very powerful weapon. That is why during Praise & Worship the enemy tries to distract the people. Their minds wander to concerns that they brought in with them. They are trying to get comfortable in their seats. Musical instruments will malfunction, microphones will squeal, whispering amongst neighbors, ushers moving around – enemy uses anything to distract the people from entering into the presence of the Lord.

But … (say **BUT!**) when the whole body moves as one into the presence of the Lord, Watch Out! Miracles are going to happen. The altar of God is open for the people to come and let their Father touch them. He knows what each person needs for that very moment.

Do you know what I am talking about? Have you noticed the hush that comes over the sanctuary, people are worshiping God then the Pastor steps up to the altar and opens the altar for prayer? Being in the Holy of Holies with God does not take a long time if the congregation wants to enter into God's presence.

My Example:

Years ago I was asked to speak for 15-20 minutes to the inmates at a juvenile detention center. All the young men were outside for the day and various singers and ministries had come that day to minister to them. This was a very fun day for the youth who are incarcerated.

The day was extremely hot and when I arrived at 5:00 p.m., the man who was organizing the event told me as I stepped onto the stage, "You have three minutes!" I was stunned, but said "okay".

I prayed saying, "Lord, You are in charge; show me what to do", and I stepped on the stage.

I put on the stereo the song, "Shout to the Lord". Right in middle of the song I felt the Holy Spirit sweep across the field and I shouted, "Men of Cheltenham stand to your feet and shout to the Lord!"

I will never forget the sight of what my God did in three minutes. Every one of those hot, tired young men jumped to their feet, shouting and praising God. The Holy Spirit was like a huge wave that swept through that field. God can move instantly, we just have to ask Him to have His way and **then get out of His way.**

The spirit of distraction is what we are praying against! We want the congregation to follow the Praise & Worship leader into the throne room. This person can have a very hard job, because most of the time, they are trying to carry the people into the presence of God on their backs. Instead of walking or dancing on their own, they (the sheep) want the praise ministry to carry them into God's presence. Pray for the singers and musicians!

You are a Soldier On The Wall! Use that sword!

Praying the Word of God:

- God watches over His Word to perform it.

- His Word does not come back void.

- Part of the armor, the Word is our sword

The most powerful weapon we have available to us is the Word of God, our sword. Pray the Word of God out loud.

Write down scriptures in a notebook ahead of time and take them with you to the prayer wall. Make a list and bring it with you, scriptures on salvation, on healing, on deliverance, on pulling down strongholds, on using the name of Jesus, on binding and loosing spirits, on praising God, Buy a book of scriptures broken down by topic; read it and bring it with you.

Jesus defeated Satan while being tempted by saying "It is written"... We too must follow His example. He is the Word made flesh!

I want you to pray *Psalm 91* out loud. Go get your Bible now. Take each verse and pray it for yourself, putting your name in each verse until you pray through this psalm.

Example:

Verse 1: Shellie, you will dwell in the shelter of the Most High, and you abide in the shadow of the Almighty.

Okay get praying. This is how you pray the Word of God.

YOUR EXAMPLE:

_____
_____
_____
_____
_____
_____
_____
_____
_____
_____
_____
_____
_____
_____
_____
_____
_____
_____
_____
_____
_____
_____
_____
_____
_____
_____
_____

Praying a cloud of protection:

        •*Exodus 14:19-24* (The enemy cannot come through it, it is the glory of God.)

Praying a hedge of protection:

        •*Job 1:10* (Assured protection around us that the enemy cannot break thru without God's permission.)

There are many other scriptures about the cloud of God and about a hedge of protection that God puts around us. (Search them out in the Word.)

Example:

Father, I ask that You put a cloud of protection around me that the enemy cannot come through in Jesus' name. Father, I pray a hedge of protection around Pastor that the enemy cannot penetrate to touch Your prophet, in Jesus' name.

YOUR EXAMPLE:

_____
_____
_____
_____
_____
_____
_____
_____
_____
_____
_____
_____
_____
_____
_____
_____
_____
_____
_____
_____

Here is the setting:

You are on the wall, I am in the sanctuary and send you a text "Pray". What is going on?: I have seen or discerned that the enemy is in the sanctuary.

How are you going to pray? Cloud or Hedge?

Why?

_____
_____
_____
_____
_____
_____
_____
_____

What should your prayer partner be doing?: Looking at the security camera to see where the attack is coming from, listening to your prayer and being in agreement with what you are praying.

At this point, we are a three-stranded cord that is not easily broken. We are praying protection for the Pastor, because he/she will be the enemy's target.

Pleading the Blood of Jesus:

On the first Passover, the top of the door and both doorposts were marked with the blood of a Lamb and the plague of death did not touch them [*Exodus 12:1-30*]

We are also washed/marked by the blood of the Lamb (Jesus) when we pray for salvation.

The enemy hates the blood of Jesus because it reminds him of his defeat. Jesus while on the cross was the perfect blood sacrifice. He said, "It is finished!" (Meaning literally, paid in full!)

We are redeemed (saved from sin) and justified (made right before God) by the blood of Jesus. Only by the shedding of Jesus' blood could we be made right with God.

The enemy hates the blood of Jesus because it reminds him of his defeat. (Yes, I know I repeated this sentence, I want it imbedded into your heart and mind.)

Example:

While praying I have seen in visions on many occasions thousands of demons lined up and advancing. I have bound them in the name of Jesus, but I saw that though they were tied they were still moving forward. But when I applied the Blood of Jesus, they were shattered. The blood of Jesus appeared to me to be like an acid bomb against them. You can remind them that the Blood of Jesus is against them and they will back off. Use His name and His blood.

Here is an example how to use the blood of Jesus in a prayer:

Father,
 I lift sister (so and so) up to You, I plead the blood of Jesus over her to wash away every sickness that is being used against her because no weapon formed against her shall prosper. By the stripes You took Jesus she is healed. By and through Jesus I pray. Amen.

Here is another example:

I apply the blood of Jesus over my finances and I command every spirit that has an assignment against me to loose my finances in Jesus' mighty name.

The Name of Jesus:

•Cast out demons in Jesus name [*Matthew 7:22*]

•Do miracles in Jesus name [*Mark 9:39*]

•Demonics must listen and obey in His name [*Luke 10:17*]

•Ask the Father in the name of Jesus [*John 15:16 & 16:26*]

•No other name under heaven given to men by which we must be saved (like Jesus) [*Acts 4:12*]

Every time we pray, we go to the Father through the Son and the Holy Spirit gives us the words to pray. All Three persons are involved in our prayers. There is no other name in heaven or earth that is like Jesus'. As children of God we are given permission to use His name. Demons do not obey us as individuals, but only obey us when using the name of Jesus because of His authority.

Anointing Oil:

• *James 5:14* (used to anoint the sick)

•Used to anoint objects that were dedicated to be used in the holy place

•Used to anoint and appoint positions in the church

Anointing oil was first mentioned in the Old Testament. God told the priests how to make special anointing oil that was to be used only for ministry. The New Testament tells us to anoint the sick, lay hands on the sick and pray. Bodies were anointed for burial. Jesus said the woman with the alabaster jar pre-anointed him for burial. The women after Jesus died went to the tomb to (prepare) anoint His body; **BUT** He wasn't there! Praise God, He had risen from the grave!

We use oil to anoint doorways, to symbolize the anointment of the doorposts for Passover. We anoint to symbolize the blood of Jesus, like a line drawn in the sand that the enemy cannot cross. There is not anything special in oil; but when you pray and ask God to use it as Anointing Oil only to be used for ministry, in the spirit realm the enemy takes notice and listens and watches us as to how you are going to use it. It is made holy unto the Lord. From my experience, the enemy sees it as the Blood of the Lamb.

When I go to pray for someone or go to spiritually cleanse a home, this is one of the many weapons I always have with me. I take my Bible, I wear a cross, I take Holy Water and Anointing Oil. The Holy Spirit will guide you as to how to use these weapons against the enemy.

If you don't have anointing oil, you can go to a Christian bookstore and purchase a bottle or you can buy Olive Oil. Pour some in a small bottle and then you can carry it in your purse (for ladies) or your pants pocket (for men).

You can purchase a plastic bottle from a Christian Bookstore that is printed "Holy Water" on it. You will fill this container with water. Water was used and is still used for cleansing. When we are saved we are cleansed of our sins by the blood Jesus shed for us on the cross. Once again, in my experience, the enemy sees Holy Water as the blood of Jesus.

This is an example of what you might pray to dedicate your bottle of Anointing Oil or Holy Water, hold the bottle in your hand as you pray:

Father,
I dedicate this bottle of Anointing Oil/Holy Water to be used for Your glory in ministry. I ask that You bless it and direct me as to how and when to use it. I anoint myself right now as a minister in Your service. In Jesus' name I pray. Amen.

Whatever other weapons God instructs you to bring onto the battlefield, you can dedicate in the same way.

NOTES:

_____

_____

_____

_____

_____

_____

_____

_____

_____

_____

_____

_____

_____

_____

_____

_____

_____

_____

_____

_____

_____

_____

_____

_____

_____

_____

_____

_____

_____

Reminder: Pray now before moving onto the next chapter.

Chapter 17 - Defensive Weaponry

These are some of the weapons we can use to defend ourselves in a spiritual battle:

The Sword – The Word of God:

We have already discussed the Sword, and how important the Word of God is in every spiritual battle.

Shield of Faith:

The shield of faith is used to block anything shot at us or thrown at us.

Applying the Blood of Jesus:

Applying the blood of Jesus: speaking the blood of Jesus is like throwing an acid bomb on the demonic. Holy water and anointing oil represent God's holiness and the blood of Jesus.

Binding in the name of Jesus:

Memorize this verse:

Matthew 16:19 - "I will give you the keys of the kingdom of heaven; and whatever you shall bind on earth will be bound in heaven, and whatever you loose on earth will be loosed in heaven."

This verse has protected me while in battle over and over again.

Examples:

While going to lead a Bible study at a juvenile detention center, I found myself standing in the middle of two very angry young men ready to tear each other apart and I had nowhere to go. I looked directly in the eyes (the eyes are lamp into the soul) of the one standing in front of me and I bound that spirit of anger in the name of Jesus and commanded it to back off. It did and the young men turned and walked away. Praise God, no blood shed, mine or theirs.

At another time I walked into that same facility and a young man who was demon possessed yelled as soon as I walked into the room, "We don't want you here!" Once again, I bound that demon and told it that it must be silent in the name of Jesus. The young man sat down.

Loosing in the name of Jesus:

Examples:

While praying and interceding for a family under spiritual attack, I saw a vision of a dragon coming at me shooting fire. I said, "I bind you in the name of Jesus", and the Lord spoke to me and said finish the verse! I then said, "I loose the fire from the throne of God in the name of Jesus", and a huge fireball was flung from heaven and struck the dragon and it was burnt up.

Many times I have prayed to loose the archangels to join me in battle.

I pray every night for the Lord to loose His angels to surround me as I sleep.

Jesus gave us this right to loose when he said he gave us the keys of heaven. Jesus is the key to everything. He gave us this key when He died for us. The Holy Spirit lives in us; He is the One that has told me to finish the verse time and again. He is right with you in battle, telling you what to do and pray. The battle and victory belong to Him.

Whatever we read in the Word that was used by God's people was sent from God in the past, we can loose in warfare today. He is the same yesterday, today and tomorrow.

Arrows:

There are many types of arrows:

Arrows From Heaven:

Job 6:4 - *"The arrows of the Almighty are in me..*

Job 16:13 - *"his archers surround me..."*

Psalm 18:14 - *"He shot his arrow and scattered the enemy,..."*

Arrows From Ourselves:

Jeremiah 9:8 - *"Their tongue is a deadly arrow; It speaks deceitfully...he sets a trap for him."*

So our tongue when used to speak the Word against the enemy is like a deadly arrow, it pierces. It sets an ambush so no weapon formed against us will prosper, or come into completion.

The Enemy Shoots Arrows:

Psalm 11:2 - *"For look, behold, the wicked bend their bows; they set their arrow against the strings to shoot from the shadows at the upright in heart"*

Psalm 76:3 - *"There he broke the flashing arrows, the shields and the swords, the weapons of war."*

Example:

While interceding during a class, I saw a person enter and (I saw in the spirit) there was an arrow sticking out of their back. The person sat next to me and I laid my hand on their knee and prayed that the Lord would remove the arrow. People walk around spiritually wounded by the enemy not realizing they need prayer for healing.

Fire from God:

1 Kings 18:38 - *"Then the fire of the Lord fell and burned up the sacrifice, the wood, the stones and the soil, and also licked up the water in the trench."*

Jeremiah 23:29 - *"Is not my word like fire,' declares the Lord and like a hammer that breaks a rock in pieces?'"*

Exodus 3:2 - *"There the angel of the Lord appeared to him in flames of fire from within the bush…"*

Hail:

Exodus 9:18 - *"Therefore, at this time tomorrow I will send the worst hailstorm that has ever fallen on Egypt, from the day it was founded till now."*

Joshua 10:11 - *"As they fled before Israel on the road down from Beth Horon to Azekah, the Lord hurled large hailstones down on them, and more of them died from the hail than were killed by the swords of the Israelites."*

Revelation 16:21 - *"From the sky huge hailstones, each weighing about a hundred pounds, fell on people. And they cursed God on account of the plague of hail, because the plague was so terrible."*

Stones, Sling & Staff (Stick):

1 Samual 17:40 - *"Then he took his staff in his hand, chose five smooth stones from the steam, put them in the pouch of his shepherd's bag and, with his sling in his hand, approached the Philistine."*

Mark 6:8 - *"These were his instructions: 'Take nothing for the journey except a staff—no bread, no bag, no money in your belts.'"*

Acts 7:59 - *"While they were stoning him, Stephen prayed, Lord Jesus, receive my spirit.'"*

Stones were used to kill people in the Biblical times. They were thrown by hand or a sling was used for projection. Stephen was stoned and the adulterous woman was going to be stoned.

Ax:

Psalm 74:6 - *"They smashed all the carved paneling with their axes and hatchets."*

Jeremiah 46:22 - *"Egypt will hiss like a fleeing serpent as the enemy advances in force; they will come against her with axes, like men who cut down trees."*

Matthew 3:10 - *"The ax is already at the root of the trees; and every tree that does not produce good fruit will be cut down and thrown into the fire."*

Any weapon you read about in the Bible can be used in battle at the direction of the Holy Spirit; **BUT** (say BUT!) you must read the Bible to know what is available.

NOTES:

_____

_____

_____

_____

_____

_____

_____

_____

_____

_____

_____

_____

_____

_____

_____

_____

_____

_____

_____

_____

_____

_____

_____

_____

_____

_____

_____

_____

Reminder: Pray now before moving onto the next chapter.

Chapter 18 - Signs Of The Enemy

Here are a few signs that the enemy may be present:

•Sensing the enemy's presence or seeing the enemy.

•Distractions in the sanctuary.

•People talking, not entering into worship, babies crying, unnecessary movement in the sanctuary.

•Pastor loses his/her voice or loses his/her place while reading. Any sign of distress when he/she is preaching.

•Electronics malfunction.

Check the video feed and one person with eyes open watch the congregation for disturbances and unusual expressions and behavior. You can be praying in agreement with your partner, while watching.

We must be on alert while standing watch on the wall. Watch for unusual signs and if they appear, use your weapons to force the enemy to leave the building. All Soldiers On The Wall come together in agreement in prayer.

You may be wondering, "Why?"

Ecclesiastes 4:12 - *"Though one may be overpowered, two can defend themselves. A cord of three strands is not quickly broken."*

Matthew 18:20 - *"For where two or three gather in my name, there am I with them."*

Deuteronomy 32:30-31 - *"How could one man chase a thousand, or two put ten thousand to flight, unless their Rock had sold them, unless the Lord had given them up? For their rock is not like our Rock, as even our enemies concede."*

My vision is to have at the minimum of three soldiers on duty in every Pastor's office and one in every sanctuary for every service. The more you see victory, the hungrier you are going to be to see souls saved.

If you haven't signed up for a certain service to stand on the wall, but in your spirit you know you need to be there, go **and join the soldiers!** The Holy Spirit is prompting you.

Every soldier needs to attend a service. If you have two or more services on a Sunday, attend one and stand the wall for another. If you have one service, stand the wall every other week. You must be fed and watered to have strength to stand.

NOTES:

_____
_____
_____
_____
_____
_____
_____
_____
_____
_____
_____
_____
_____
_____
_____
_____
_____
_____
_____
_____
_____
_____
_____
_____

Reminder: Pray now before moving onto the next chapter.

Chapter 19 - How Do I Approach The Wall For Duty?

Before you enter the church:

Check each piece of your armor of God.

Anoint yourself.

Ask God to increase in you and that you would be decreased to be an effective soldier for His glory.

Pray before you report for duty.

Have a list of scriptures ready to use.

Attend Praise & Worship

You must prepare yourself before you come on duty. I cannot stress this enough, give your problems to the Lord to clear your mind.

You now have anointing oil; anoint yourself. Wear some sign of the cross, be it a cross or a prayer shawl embellished with a cross. **Show the enemy your colors.** Raise your banner. You represent Jesus. The enemy recognizes the authority of the cross. They also know if you are a threat or not.

The singers always go out before the soldiers. Attend Praise & Worship, sit in the back and quietly slip out at the end. Pray to assist the ushering in of the presence of the Lord. If you see disturbances, slip out and go into the office and start praying.

After Praise & Worship, go into your Pastor's office (or wherever you have agreed to pray) and shut the door with your prayer partner(s). Welcome the Holy Spirit to fill the church and ask Him to direct you on how to pray. Have your Bible open and ready to use.

Pray that your church would draw the lost and hurting as a safe house in your city.

When your Pastor begins to close in prayer strongly intercede that the lost would be saved, that God would soften their hard hearts to receive Him as Savior. Whatever reason the Pastor is opening the altar for, intercede for that specific need.

Remember, you may be able to be heard in the sanctuary, so keep your voices down. You do not need to shout; the enemy can hear a whisper. He cannot read your mind, so you have to use your voice in battle.

Ask the Lord to direct you in prayer. If the enemy enters the building, the Holy Spirit will direct you in how to send it out of the building. Trust God, it is His battle.

Alternate praying with your partner. One will watch the cameras, while the other prays out loud so that the watcher can be in agreement with you; then you will switch off, as led by the Holy Spirit.

<u>No silent prayer on the wall!</u> This is not private time with the Lord; this is guard duty. No IPod while on duty; you have to be able to hear what is going on in the sanctuary and agree with your partner. You have already been in Praise & Worship; you are ready for battle.

I cannot stress this enough, **NO** "Lone Rangers" on the wall.

There is a time for individual prayer and worship. On wall duty you are working as a troop of soldiers and you depend on your fellow soldiers in battle.

You can hear what is going on in the sanctuary, so use your ears to obtain direction from your Pastor.

You have the ability to see throughout the whole building by utilizing the security cameras. Be like spies on the wall, watching and praying.

The singers have already gone out before you, now you are ready to intercede.

Pray that the glory of God would fill the church from the sanctuary reaching through to all the classrooms.

Pray that all gifts of the Holy Spirit would be manifested in your church for the edification of the body of Christ.

Pray for protection over everyone who has come into the church that day.

Pray for the Children's Church staff.

Pray that all servants would move as one body for God's glory.

Pray that the sick would be healed.

Pray that any chain binding someone would be removed; deliverance from whatever binds them.

Pray that the sheep would be fed.

Pray for revelation knowledge of the Word of God for your Pastor.

Pray that God would open the eyes of your Pastor and he/she would be able to see the needs of the sheep.

Pray when the Pastor is approaching the altar call that the spirit of distraction would be silent. Bind it in the name of Jesus! This is when the enemy loves to show himself. If he can distract the people, they will not listen to the Spirit of the Lord calling them to the altar.

Pray for whatever reason the altar call of that Pastor is being made -- pray specifically that people would come forward and that pride/fear would not hinder them. Pray that hard hearts would be softened.

These are just a few of the things you want God to do in your church. Pray as He leads you. Glorify the Lord; thank Him for being your God. Praise Him; He inhabits the praises of His people.

Remember praise is a weapon.

Use a prayer journal that should be kept where your Soldiers On The Wall pray. At the end of your time on the wall, sit down and record what happened during that time. So the next soldiers to come on duty know if there was a battle or not. Record for them to read if God's glory fell in the office, sanctuary or classrooms. Write your observations! Write the scriptures you were led to pray. This will confirm this ministry to your Pastor, who will be monitoring the prayer journal. This also will help Pastor and your leader of Soldiers On The Wall to know if the wall needs to be reinforced during certain services.

Basically trust God and pray!

Use the "Note" section to write some of the tactics the enemy is using against your church so that you can prepare some scriptures for battle on the wall.

NOTES:

_____

_____

_____

_____

_____

_____

_____

_____

_____

_____

_____

_____

_____

_____

_____

_____

_____

_____

_____

_____

_____

_____

_____

_____

_____

_____

_____

_____

_____

_____

_____

Reminder: Pray now before moving onto the next chapter.

Chapter 20 - Postures For Prayer

What is the right posture for prayer?

NO WAY IS WRONG!

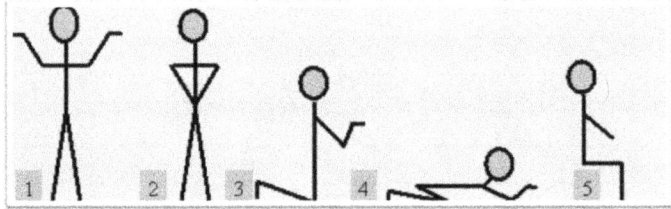

•Sitting
•Kneeling
• Prostrate on the floor
•Walking or pacing
•Stomping your foot
•Standing and swaying
•Sitting and rocking
•Hands lifted in prayer
•Clapping
•Face lifted to Heaven
•Eyes open
•Eyes closed
•Dancing
•Shouting

There are so many postures for prayer; no way is wrong. Do whatever you feel led to do. There are times when the glory of God is so strong, that you will not be able to stand and you will find yourself on your face on the floor.

If you feel the need to shout, please take it outside, but tell security first. God's service is always done in orderly manner and shouting in nearby room would cause chaos in the Sanctuary; definitely not of God. There is a time and place to shout so listen to the leading of God.

NOTES:

_____
_____
_____
_____
_____
_____
_____
_____
_____
_____
_____
_____
_____
_____
_____
_____
_____
_____
_____
_____
_____
_____
_____
_____
_____

Reminder: Pray now before moving onto the next chapter.

Chapter 21 - Fasting

Fasting is an incredible prayer discipline, tool and weapon that God uses to move us into position for Him to move. It is not **if** you will fast, but **when** you will fast. God can call you into a fast, a leader can call a fast or you may feel a personal desperation to fast.

What does fasting mean:

It means to give up something important to you for a set period of time. The most common thing is to give up food and certain types of drinks. Some people fast television or computer time, anything you would normally do that is not spent as time with God. Married couples, by mutual consent, may abstain from marital relations.

Use the time you would have been eating or whatever else you are giving up, by devoting that time to prayer and spending time listening to God.

No one likes to fast, the flesh will fight against it all the way.

The first time God told me to fast; I didn't even know what it meant. I called my sister, Susan, in New Orleans and asked her what did this mean. She explained fasting and then mailed a book on fasting to me by over-night mail.

My first fast was liquid lasting only three days. I made the *mistake* of eating a huge meal after this fast. I stress *mistake*. Your body will not be ready for a heavy meal after an extended fast; take it easy. Gradually go back to solid food.

Some Benefits of Fasting:

•Some demons can only be removed by fasting and prayer. **[Mark 9:29]**

•Enemy attacks can be cancelled. *[Esther 4:15, 7:3-6]*

•Entire groups of people can be saved. *[Esther 4:16]*

•Hear from God. *[Exodus 34:28, Isaiah 58]*

•Given direction in ministry. *[Deuteronomy 4:29]*

•Territory held by the enemy taken back for the Lord. *[2 Samuel 8]*

Types of Fasts:

Normal Fast:

No food, only water.

and

Absolute Fast:

No food or water *[Acts 9:9]*

Jesus fasted 40 days *[Luke 4:2]*

The Bible gives examples of no more than three days for this type of fast. The body can go without food for a long time, but not water and sleep. Unless God absolutely calls you into this type of fast longer (as was the cases of Moses and Elijah,) this type of fast is for extreme emergencies.

Ezra 10:6 (One day)

Queen Esther, *[Esther 4:16]* (three days to save entire group of people)

Paul, [*Acts 9:9*] (three days to restore his sight)

Supernatural Fast

Moses, (*Deuteronomy 9:9, 18; Exodus 34:28*) (In the presence of God for 40 days and nights. Ten Commandments given then immediately another 40 days after the betrayal of people, he went back to the mountain another 40 days - 80 days total longest fast in Bible.)

Elijah, [*1Kings 19:8*] (40 days and nights)

Moses and Elijah were kept supernaturally by God during these times.

Partial Fast:

Abstain from certain foods or drinks, restricting your diet.

Daniel Fast

[*Daniel 10:2-3*] (they ate vegetables and water for three week.)

Elijah, [*1 Kings 17*] (the Lord provided him bread and meat both morning and night. He drank water. In the widow's home given simple cakes of meal and oil)

Partial fast is used when Absolute Fast is impossible because of work or health reasons. God still honors this kind of fast.

I have fasted many different ways; in whatever way I have committed to fasting, God has honored them all.

God sees your heart and loves when you come aside seeking Him in earnest. If you seek Him, you will find Him.

Your Soldiers On The Wall should be fasting as a troop of soldiers committed to holding and expanding the spiritual wall of your church. Who should call a corporate fast? Your leader, your Pastor!

You may want to ask me; "Shellie, what if I mess up and eat or drink something I committed to give up?" My answer, "Your spirit is willing but the body is weak. Pray and ask God to forgive you and continue your fast."

Pray and ask God how you should fast, He knows you best.

There are many books devoted to the discipline of fasting, purchase a few and read further on this powerful tool.

NOTES:

_____
_____
_____
_____
_____
_____
_____
_____
_____
_____
_____
_____
_____
_____
_____
_____
_____
_____
_____
_____
_____

Reminder: Pray now before moving onto the next chapter.

Chapter 22 - The Enemy Is Made Up Like An Army

Where did Satan and demons come from?

Satan was a beautiful archangel and was jealous of God, he wanted God's glory. A battle broke out in heaven and Satan and 1/3 of Heaven's angels that followed him were thrown out of Heaven. Satan's followers are demons.

•Leader: Satan

•Demons: fallen angels that follow their leader. They rank in power like a military. They can appear as angels of light; but there is no light of God in them. They are darkness. False gods are higher ranking demons. *[Ephesian 6:12; Colossians 2:15; 1 Peter 3:22; 2 Corinthians 11:14]*

Revelation 12: 7-12

"Then war broke out in heaven. Michael and his angels fought against the dragon, and the dragon and his angels fought back. But he was not strong enough, and they lost their place in heaven. The great dragon was hurled down—that ancient serpent called the devil, or Satan, who leads the whole world astray. He was hurled to the earth, and his angels with him. Then I heard a loud voice in heaven say: 'Now have come the salvation and the power and the kingdom of our God, and the authority of his Messiah. For the accuser of our brothers and sisters, who accuses them before our God day and night, has been hurled down. They triumphed over him by the blood of the Lamb and by the word of their testimony; they did not love their lives so much as to shrink from death. Therefore rejoice, you heavens and you who dwell in them! But woe to the earth and the sea, because the devil has gone down to you! He is filled with fury, because he knows that his time is short.'"

Luke 10:17-20

"The seventy-two returned with joy and said, 'Lord, even the demons submit to us in your name.' He replied, 'I saw Satan fall like lightning from heaven. I have given you authority to trample on snakes and scorpions and to overcome all the power of the enemy; nothing will harm you. However, do not rejoice that the spirits submit to you, but rejoice that your names are written in heaven.'"

We cannot kill a demon. In my visions they explode. God's way of removing them from an attack, but definitely not dead just gone.

We can make them flee in the name of Jesus.

Every demon was defeated by the work of Jesus on the cross. His shed blood and His resurrection defeated them.

Their time is limited; time is short.

I have personally seen six levels of this demonic army during an eleven-week spiritual battle on behalf of a family member I have ministered to. As one demon was defeated, a stronger one was sent until the battle stopped. This family continues to have attacks once in a while, but have learned how to stop the battle before it rages again. Demons will try to return to where they were thrown out of, but if the house is clean, they cannot re-enter.

Matthew 12:43-45

"When an impure spirit comes out of a person, it goes though arid places seeking rest and does not find it. Then it says, 'I will return to the house I left.' When it arrives, it finds the house unoccupied, swept clean and put in order. Then it goes and takes with it seven other spirits more wicked than itself, and they go in and live there. And the final condition of that person is worse than the first. That is how it will be with this wicked generation."

Ephesians 6:12

"For our struggle is not against flesh and blood, but against the rulers, against the authorities, against the powers of this dark world and against the spiritual forces of evil in the heavenly realms."

Demons can change shape to instill FEAR. Number one weapon used against us.

Examples:

Snake in the Garden of Eden. *[Genesis 3:1-5]*

Dragon in the book of Revelation. *[Revelation 12:9]*

But God did not give us a spirit of fear but of POWER and a SOUND Mind. *[2 Timothy 1:7]*

The battle is the Lord's. Therefore, when we are attacked, the enemy is attacking the Lord since He lives in us.

We are created in God's image that is why demons hate us so much. Jesus told us to use His name it reminds the enemy that he cannot win. He must flee.

John 8:44

"You belong to your father, the devil, and you want to carry out your father's desires. He was a murderer from the beginning, not holding to the truth, for there is no truth in him. When he lies, he speaks his native language, for he is a liar and the father of lies."

2 Corinthians 11:14

"And no wonder, for Satan himself masquerades as an angel of light."

1 Peter 5:8

"Be alert and of sober mind. Your enemy the devil prowls around like a roaring lion looking for someone to devour."

Jude 1:9

"But even the archangel Michael, when he was disputing with the devil about the body of Moses, did not himself dare to condemn him for slander but said, 'The Lord rebuke you!'"

James 4:7

"Submit yourselves, then, to God. Resist the devil, and he will flee from you."

Ephesians 4:27

"and do not give the devil a foothold."

NOTES:

_____

_____

_____

_____

_____

_____

_____

_____

_____

_____

_____

_____

_____

_____

_____

_____

_____

_____

_____

_____

_____

_____

_____

_____

_____

_____

_____

_____

_____

_____

_____

_____

_____

Reminder: Pray now before moving onto the next chapter.

Chapter 23 - Territorial Spirits

We touched a little on the subject of territorial spirits in previous chapters. My understanding of the subject is this:

There are demons assigned to oppress a person. (Lowest demon in rank.)

There is a higher level to oppress a race of people, the same level to oppress generations of a family. Also known as "generational curses".

There are levels that go up:

    •City

    •State

    •Country

Think in the terms of army and ranks. And within each level can be many sublevels according to strength.

Mark 13:25

"and the stars will fall from the sky, and the heavenly bodies will be shaken."

Luke 21:26

"People will faint from terror, apprehensive of what is coming on the world, for the heavenly bodies will be shaken."

Romans 8:38-39

"For I am convinced that neither death nor life, neither angels nor demons, neither the present nor the future, nor any powers, neither height nor depth, nor anything else in all creation, will be able to separate us from the love of God that is in Christ Jesus our Lord."

Ephesians 6:12

"For our struggle is not against flesh and blood, but against the rulers, against the authorities, against the powers of this dark world and against the spiritual forces of evil in the heavenly realms."."

1 Peter 3:21-22

"and this water symbolizes baptism that now saves you also—not the removal of dirt from the body but the pledge of a clear conscience toward God. It saves you by the resurrection of Jesus Christ, who has gone into heaven and is at God's right hand—with angels, authorities and powers in submission to him."

We don't need to know their names; we just need to know their assignment to break their hold on us.

Example:

In my family, on both my maternal and paternal sides, there had been participation in the highest-levels of masons. When I researched this I realized that this is a satanic group. I asked one of my sisters to come and pray with me to break the oaths and curses that were pledged against our family through past generations. We were under spiritual attack the whole time that we were praying, but we got through the prayer. Those curses were broken off from us. God will reveal to you if you need to pray any similar prayers.

God is the only One who can reveal to us who the enemy is, what his assignment is and the battle plan. To take a territory back from the enemy takes fasting and prayer.

Every battle in the Bible that was won, was won by taking direction for the battle strategy from God. You **never** remove a territorial demon until God gives you a battle plan.

We are not to fear the enemy! It seems a huge task, but just think, only a third of the angels were thrown down to earth.

How much bigger is the army of God! He has already won the victory. We are part of His army, and we fight for those who cannot fight or do not know who to fight or how to fight.

Once again, I must stress to you that our God is bigger and stronger than any power and principality that we may have discussed. Every battle that I have ever engaged in, God has always won.

The only time I can think of that a person still had a demonic presence in their home, was because that person refused to let go of the demon. They were deceived and believed they could continue to learn how to stand against the demonic by living in a battle zone. LIE! LIE! Satan is the father of lies!

I was saved by the experience of having a demon in my home. I had to learn real quick what I believed in and who could help me. The only person who could help me was Jesus Christ. It was a territorial demon, because the family who owned the house before me sold the house to get away from it. Because of unexplained noises, I called a psychic and which just opened the spiritual window even more. Realizing my error, I repented and prayed for salvation.

I was saved and then taught by a pastor who dealt with this how to spiritually clean my home from demons. God did not expect me to live in fear. He expected me to learn how to throw that thing out of my home and so I did.

God uses everything bad for our good. He knew the plans He had for my life and I am now walking in those plans.

A must-read book is <u>Territorial Spirits</u> by C. Peter Wagner.

Get this book!

This book is compiled of different chapters written by leaders from huge churches and ministries and how they took back a region for God.

I had so many "ah-ha" moments while reading this book; and confirmations of what I have witnessed and experienced in battle.

Let's start with a few powerful excerpts from this book:

Forward:
[Pg. 16] *"We need to lift ourselves out of a self-centered spirituality, a mentality that says we are victims rather than warriors. Fiery darts will come, but as we raise the shield of faith, we must take up the sword of the Spirit and join with others in contending for cities and nations."*

We must think even bigger than our own family and friends.

I commend each individual for taking the important step of joining or organizing a Soldiers On The Wall. God wants to take back cities and He is calling all of us to duty.

There will be times of standing and holding our ground; but there will also be times when we will be called to advance under the direction of God.

[Pg. 22] *"In recent times, the old gods have begun to show their faces again, particularly in children's entertainment...parts of the world people are openly worshipping the old territorial spirits. An example would be the renewed worship of Thor and Odin in Scandinavia and the reemergence of the druids in Britain."*

In one of my most recent battles, the Lord told me what I was seeing spiritually was ancient. These ancient elements are re-emerging because of the impending "End Times". Time is short and Satan is bringing back old tactics that have worked in the past.

Fear not! Nothing is new to God! He has a plan!

[Pg. 35] *"When Jesus came, He invaded Satan's kingdom with the Kingdom of God. Satan was not only insulted, but his power was broken through the death and resurrection of Jesus Christ. He is not taking this invasion lying down. That is why violence has erupted both in the Heavenlies and here on earth. That is why Jesus said, 'The kingdom of heaven suffers violence and the violent take it by force' Matt 11:12"*

Notice Satan's power was broken by Jesus. We are on the winning side!!! Also note Heavenlies is, plural; remember we discussed about the three levels of Heaven. Singular usage is when the throne room of God is referred to.

In Chapter 1 Wagner goes into depth about our relationship with God. We must be holy to be effective soldiers. He describes holiness as being so filled with the presence of God, there is little room for anything else.

As I stated before, you must spend time with God; that is our action. The Holy Spirit's job is to make us holy; that is God's action.

God wants to educate and change us to be effective in warfare. It is our choice on how much time we spend with God. Do you truly want to see the lost saved and to be set free from what oppresses them?

God is searching for those of us who are hungry for more of God. He will first trust you with a little before He trusts you with much. Holding the wall, little – taking the city, much! Amen?

Chapter 2 [pg. 57] *Steve Nicholson preached for 6 years with little effect, until he started fasting and praying. A demon showed up and challenged him for the city asking him why are you bothering me? He answered naming streets in the area. The demon said it was too much. Nicholson commands the demon in the name of Jesus to give up that territory.*

Notice nothing much happened until he started fasting and praying specifically for streets by name. The demon was disturbed and confronted him. He didn't ask for the whole city, he took it piece by piece. He didn't demand that the demon, he **commanded** the demon in the **name of Jesus** to give it up. We have authority to use the name of Jesus.

. "·[Pg. 62] *"Dawson differentiates between points of entry' and" dominant features' of a region. A point of entry would be a historic event, such as slave trade, that gave sin a place in the community, this enabling demonic force to establish a foothold*

When praying about territorial demons in any area, we need to look also at the history of that area. We do not need to re-create the wheel. Look at your area, major historical events. Look at major crimes in a specific area. Look at the types of businesses in the area. What exactly is the major attraction or claim to infamy for that area?

With that knowledge, start fasting and praying. asking God what is the name or the assignment in our area. How do we approach this battle? God has a plan.

[Pg. 64] *"the key to breaking spiritual strongholds is not to focus on Satan — though we can uncover the devil's work — but to focus on Jesus Christ and the power of the Holy Spirit."*

Jesus is the Key. The power of the Holy Spirit is in us. We do not want to glorify Satan and his demons for their work in an area--we want to glorify God by seeing thousands saved.

Now that is true power! The only reason we battle and take territory is so that others are set free and saved.

[Pg. 90] *"Just because we are under attack, doesn't mean we are unprotected. The loving and protective presence of God shields us moment by moment from haphazard assaults. If we sin, the indwelling Spirit immediately goes to work on our conscience to convict us of our transgression."*

This is so important. God never leaves us, He is always with us.

[Pg. 91] *"Some learning is 'caught' in the course of battle, not 'taught' in a seminar or learned through a book. Today, we need to be open to allow God to train us to see the subtleties of evil. May God be pleased to raise up men and women equipped to see as He sees, and committed to act with His authority to counteract the kingdom of darkness in our age."*

NOTES:

_____
_____
_____
_____
_____
_____
_____
_____
_____
_____
_____
_____
_____
_____
_____
_____
_____
_____
_____
_____
_____
_____
_____
_____
_____
_____
_____
_____
_____
_____
_____
_____

Reminder: Pray now before moving onto the next chapter.

Conclusion

I was going to continue but the Lord stopped me and said that now He will take over in your training. I pray that you grasp what He shows you in battle.

Be in unity with other intercessors to hold the prayer wall for your church and/or your prayer group to take territory back from the enemy.

How?

PRAYER AND MORE PRAYER!

The battle is the Lord's, and we follow Him.

Hugs & Blessings in the precious name of Jesus,

Rev. Shellie Polk

Now What?

You may be thinking, "What just happened?"

The following are the four principles stated at Encounter Christian Center in Charlotte Hall, Maryland every Sunday:

-You   (1) **ADMITTED**: That God has not been first place in your life.

> *[1 John 1:9*, *"If we confess our sins, He is faithful and just and will forgive us our sins and purify us from all unrighteousness."]*

-You   (2) **BELIEVED**: That Jesus died to pay for your sins.

> *[Romans 10:9, "If you declare with your mouth, 'Jesus is Lord,' and believe in your heart that God raise Him from the dead, you will be saved."]*

-You   (3) **ACCEPTED**: God's free gift. Don't try to earn it.

> *[Ephesians 2:8-9, "For it is by grace you have been saved, through faith—this is not from yourselves, it is the gift of God—not by works, so that no one can boast."]*

-You   (4) **INVITED**: Jesus Christ to come into your life and be Lord (the boss) of your life.

> *[John 1:12-14, "Yet to all who did receive him, to those who believed in his name, he gave the right to become children of God—children born not of natural descent, nor of human decision or a husband's will, but born of God. The Word became flesh and made his dwelling among us. We have seen his glory, the glory of the one and only Son, who came from the Father, full of grace and truth."]*

Congratulations on your decision to follow Jesus.

You have been "born again". How can that be? Your first birth was water/flesh, when you were born by your Mother (flesh) the water sack that protected you broke. The second birth just occurred. When you prayed and gave your life to Jesus and asked Him into your life, the Spirit of God entered you and He is living in you right now. The first birth is not your choice, but the second(rebirth) is your choice.

[*John 3:3-8,* *"Jesus replied, 'Very truly I tell you, no one can see the kingdom of God unless they are born again.' 'How can someone be born when they are old?' Nicodemus asked. 'Surely they cannot enter a second time into their mother's womb to be born!' Jesus answered, 'Very truly I tell you, no one can enter the kingdom of God unless they are born of water and the Spirit. Flesh gives birth to flesh, but the Spirit gives birth to spirit. You should not be surprised at my saying, 'You must be born again.' The wind blows wherever it pleases. You hear its sound, but you cannot tell where it comes from or where it is going. So it is with everyone born of the Spirit.'"*]

You have been saved from eternal death in Hell, the verdict for a sinner, and given eternal life with God in Heaven by the torture Jesus suffered on the cross out of His great love for you. This was your "salvation experience" when you prayed. Write down today's date, this is the day you were saved.

_____

[*John 3:16-18,* *"For God so loved the world that he gave his one and only Son, that whoever believes in Him shall not perish but have eternal life. For God did not send his Son into the world to condemn the world, but to save the world through Him. Whoever believes in him is not condemned, but whoever does not believe stands condemned already because they have not believed in the name of God's one and only Son."*]

All of your sins have been forgiven. You are brand new.

[*2Corinthians 5:17,* *"Therefore, if anyone is in Christ, he is a new creation; the old has gone, the new has come!"*]

When you prayed for salvation, the angels in Heaven rejoiced. A lot of angels were cheering for you.

*[**Luke 15:10,** "in the same way, I tell you, there is rejoicing in the presence of the angels of God over one sinner who repents."]*

Your name is now recorded in Jesus' Book of Life. This is the book that has a record of every person who prays for salvation.

*[**Revelation 21:27,** "Nothing impure will ever enter it, nor will anyone who does what is shameful or deceitful, but only those whose names are written in the Lamb's book of life."]*

So Now What?

Time to get to know Jesus. <u>Start reading the Bible</u>. A good place to start is with the Gospel of John found in the New Testament. (Old Testament before Jesus was born. New Testament after Jesus was born, crucified and resurrected.) Then move onto the book of Acts, which immediately follows John. (The beginning of the "church" as we know it.)

There are plenty of free Bible apps. Download the ECC app and you can listen and read along to the Bible daily. Another good app is "Bible.Is". You can select any book of the Bible and listen as you follow along in your Bible.

*[**Hebrews 4:12,** "The word of God is living and active. Sharper than any double-edged sword, it penetrates even to dividing the soul and spirit, joints and marrow; it judges the thoughts and attitudes of the heart."]*

*[**Joshua 1:8,** "Do not let this Book of the Law depart from your mouth; meditate on it day and night, so that you may be careful to do everything written in it. Then you will be prosperous and successful."]*

*[**1 Peter 2:2,** "Like newborn babies, crave pure spiritual milk, so that by it you will grow up in your salvation."]*

Start Praying!

Prayer is your communication with God. Just talk to Him, tell Him everything that is on your heart, nothing is insignificant to Him. Jesus made a way for you to come directly into the presence of God by dying on the cross. When God looks on you, He sees no sin.

[*Matthew 21:22*, *"If you believe, you will receive whatever you ask for in prayer."*]

[*John 16:23-24*, *"My Father will give you whatever you ask in my name. Until now you have not asked for anything in my name. Ask and you will receive, and your joy will be complete."*]

You might begin like this:

Father,
Thank You for _____. These are the things that I am thinking of that I cannot handle but you can: _____. Father it is written in Your Word by the stripes Jesus took on the cross, we are healed. Please heal _____. Through Jesus I thank You for listening and loving me. Amen

As you start hiding the Word of God in your heart as you read the Bible, you can start praying using the scriptures. God likes it when we pray His Word back to Him. Open your Bible as you pray and start praying the Word back to Him about situations concerning you. These are His promises to you. Look in the back of your Bible and there may be a list of subjects so that you can find the scriptures that pertain to your situation. A way to learn how to pray is to practice and by listening to others pray.

*[**John 15:7,** "If you remain in me and my words remain in you, ask whatever you wish, and it will be given you."]*

Attend Sunday Service

Find a church home. You need to hear the Word of God preached to grow from being a baby Christian into maturity. God tells us not to forsake the gathering together of the saints. There are no "Lone Ranger Christians." You need the support of your church family and we need you.

*[**Hebrew 10:24-25,** "And let us consider how we may spur one another on toward love and good deeds, not giving up meeting together, as some are in the habit of doing, but encouraging one another—and all the more as you see the Day approaching."]*

Get Connected

There are so many ways to make friends and connections at your church. Attend ministries and classes offered in your church home.

*[**1 John 1:3,7,** "We proclaim to you what we have seen and heard, so that you also may have fellowship with us. And our fellowship is with the Father and with his Son, Jesus Christ. But if we walk in the light, as he is in the light, we have fellowship with one another, and the blood of Jesus, his Son, purifies us from all sin."]*

*[**Colossians 3:16,** "Let the message of Christ dwell among you richly as you teach and admonish one another with all wisdom through psalms, hymns, and songs from the Spirit, singing to God with gratitude in your hearts."]*

[*Galatians 6:2,10,* "*Carry each other's burdens, and in this way you will fulfill the law of Christ. Therefore, as we have opportunity, let us do good to all people, especially to those who belong to the family of believers.*"]

Get Baptized

Sign up for baptism at the next Baptism service. This will be your first act of obedience as a new believer. It is your public confession of what you believe. Baptism does not save you! Your decision to pray and give your life to Jesus saved you. Baptism is an act of obedience.

[*Acts 22:14-16,* "*The God of our ancestors has chosen you to know his will and to see the Righteous One and to hear words from his mouth. You will be His witness to all people of what you have seen and heard. And now what are you waiting for? Get up, be baptized and wash your sins away, calling on His name.*"]

[*Acts 19:5,* "*On hearing this, they were baptized in the name of the Lord Jesus.*"]

[*Galatians 3:26-27,* "*So in Christ Jesus you are all children of God through faith, for all of you who were baptized into Christ have clothed yourselves with Christ.*"]

Attend New Believers Class

This class will explain what your church body believes and what the vision of your church is for the future.

Join The Membership Of Your Church

Become an official member, don't be an "Orphan Christian". Join the family!

Get Involved

Ask your Pastor what can you do to serve others as Jesus did. You have talents that God has gifted you, use them for His glory, and don't hide them. The Body needs you.

[1 Corinthians 3:5 & 9, "What, after all, is Apollos? And what is Paul? Only servants, through whom you came to believe—as the Lord has assigned to each his task. For we are co-workers in God's service; you are God's field, God's building."]

I am sure you are going to have a lot of questions in your daily walk with Jesus. That is wonderful. Take all your questions to God first through prayer and then to your church for support.

Welcome to the family of Jesus. You are brand new and nothing is impossible for you now that Jesus is leading you.

Hugs & Blessings in the Wonderful name of Jesus,

Rev. Shellie Polk

About The Author

Rev. Shellie Polk:

I was born September 24, 1960 and raised in Oxon Hill, Maryland, U.S.A. I am one of six children born to loving parents, Harry and Autumn Kraft. I met my husband when I was 9 years old and told my mother that he was who I was going to marry.

I graduated from Oxon Hill High School and then The Washington School for Secretaries. Was married May 19, 1979 to Donald Polk. I have two living children, April Buckler (married to husband, Brian Buckler and have twin granddaughters, Summer & Autumn) and Craig Polk (married to wife, Katie Polk and have four granddaughters, Danielle, Natalie, Brittney & Haley and one grandson, Sean) and I have one deceased son, Donald Polk, Jr. residing in Heaven.

I was saved in 1989 after experiencing the negative ramifications of getting involved with a psychic and after purchasing a home that had a demon residing in it. I learned real fast in what I believed and learned how to cleanse my home.

In August 1993 I was filled with the Holy Spirit at a Women's Aglow prayer meeting, then joined Calvary Gospel Church of Waldorf, Maryland in August 1993. Volunteered at the local Women's Aglow book table and tape ministry October 1993-August 1995.

May 5, 1994 the Lord opened a ministry for me entitled The Joy Concert Ministries. I have led many Praise & Worship Services at Calvary Gospel Church and Women's Aglow. Was water baptized during a Rodney Howard Brown revival at Evangel Church in Upper Marlboro, Maryland October 1994.

Was the Choir Director for the Children's Choir and was Children's Minister at Calvary Gospel Church from October 1994-1997. Was the Recording Secretary for Women's Aglow from November 1994-March 1995.

Ministered at Cheltenham Youth Facility from 1993 until January 2006. I have ministered in many nursing homes, shelters and private homes.

Graduated from Logos Bible College with an Associate Degree in Biblical Studies August 1998. Was licensed as a Minister in 1995 at Calvary Gospel Church February 1998.

I am part business owner along with my husband of an HVAC company, Multi-Aire Corp. since August 2000.

Started attending Encounter Christian Center December 2006 and became a member August 2007.

I was ordained on September 14, 2009 through Logos International Ministries.

Starting in January 2007, Donald and I led the Praise & Worship monthly for Women's Aglow for a couple of years. We held weekly Praise & Worship/Healing Services for 18 months at my brother-in-law Donnie Stallings' home (until he went home to be with our Lord, after succumbing to cancer.)

I officiate at funerals and weddings. I go into people's homes to cleanse them from being oppressed by the demonic. I pray for those under demonic attack and teach them how to defend themselves. I am reachable by phone 24/7 to take calls for prayer.

I am currently on the Ministerial Staff at Encounter Christian Center in Charlotte Hall, Maryland. The Soldiers On The Wall ministry was birthed at ECC.

God uses me predominately through prophecy and visions. It has been my great honor to pray with thousands for salvation. I have given away thousands of Bibles (generously donated by fellow believers). My heart is burdened for the unsaved and the oppressed. I am called as an Evangelist, highly-skilled in spiritual warfare.

My current assignment is to train prayer warriors into becoming elite Soldiers On The Wall. Time is short. I am to help equip other Christians learning how to lead the lost into salvation before the soon coming of our Lord Jesus Christ.

Website: www.shelliepolk.com
Email: Shellie@shelliepolk.com

www.ingramcontent.com/pod-product-compliance
Lightning Source LLC
Chambersburg PA
CBHW032103080426
42733CB00006B/404